VILLAGE TALES

The Story of Scalby
and its Residents

VILLAGE TALES

The Story of Scalby and its Residents

Alan Whitworth

ALAN SUTTON

First published in the United Kingdom in 1993 by
Alan Sutton Publishing Ltd · Phoenix Mill · Far Thrupp · Stroud · Gloucestershire

First published in the United States of America in 1993 by
Alan Sutton Publishing Inc · 83 Washington Street · Dover · NH 03820

British Library Cataloguing in Publication Data

A catalogue record for this book is available from the British Library.

ISBN 0 7509 0347 3

Library of Congress Cataloging in Publication Data applied for

Jacket Illustration: Scalby Mills; *an engraving published by T. Taylor & Son, from a painting by Hornibrook, dated 1897.*

Typeset in 10/12 Times.
Typesetting and origination by
Alan Sutton Publishing Limited.
Printed in Great Britain by
The Bath Press, Bath, Avon.

Contents

Dedicated to
Alma
My Loving Wife
who drove me there
and patiently endured my research

and

In memory of
Florence Mildred & Henry Francis Kidd, of Scalby.

To serve the interests of science, the subject of a local history should be judiciously chosen as well as patiently investigated; that place or district must afford an adequate proportion of interesting material and the central point on which they are made to bear must possess sufficient respectability to entitle it to that distinction.

George Young
A History of Whitby and Streoneshalh Abbey, 1817

LIST OF SUBSCRIBERS

Jane Armstrong, Scalby
Norman Atkinson, Scalby
Mrs E.W. Baikie, Scalby
Mrs Molly Barker, Scalby
Mrs T.A. Barton, Scalby
Mrs J. Bayes, Scalby
Mrs S.E. Bower, Scalby
Miss M.J. Bowman, Scalby
Mrs Constance Mary Boyes, Scalby
Mr E. Boyes, Newby (2 copies)
John G. Bradley, Scalby
Miss Marjorie Briggs, Newby
R.W. Chamberlin, Scarborough
P.N. Chouler, Harwood Dale
Bryan Coates, Scarborough
Cober Hill Guest House, Cloughton
James T. Crawford, Scalby
W.J. Dawson, Scalby
Mrs P.M. Dring, Scalby
Derek Egan, Nags Head Inn, Scalby
Mrs S. Frith, Aberdeen
Patricia M. Gilbert, Lewes, East Sussex
Mr J.A. Gillings, Scalby

Mrs Hilary Gray, Scalby
Richard Grunwell, Scalby
Mrs M. Hardcastle, Scalby
Michael & Jenny Hunt, Scalby
J. Martin Johnson, JP, BA, Scalby
Mrs Valerie Kirby, Pudsey
Mr & Mrs C.J.R. Locking, Scalby
Mrs E. Lyall, Snaiton
Mrs J. Mallon, Scalby
Mr & Mrs D. Marsden, Scalby
Mrs L.M. MacDonald, Taunton,
   Somerset
James H. Masterman, Scalby
Mrs S.A. McIntyre, Scalby
Mrs L. Milburn, Scalby
A.C. Milnes, Scalby
North Yorkshire County Libraries
W. Overton, Ballymena, Co. Antrim
Mrs E. Poyner, Scalby
Mrs D. Procter, Scarborough
Dr J.D. Rickinson, Scalby
Mrs K. Robinson, Scalby
J.P. Robson, Scalby

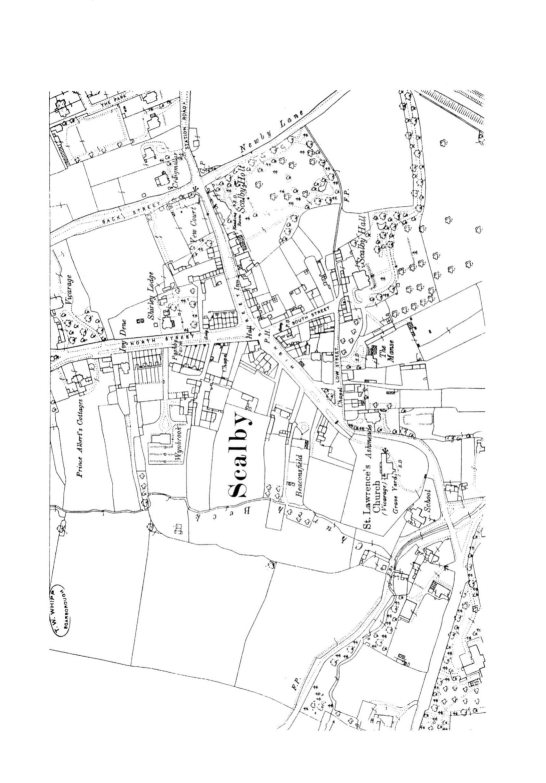

Florence Mildred 'Milly' Kidd (1901–79)

Introduction

On 30 November 1979 Miss Florence Mildred Kidd died peacefully in Scarborough hospital. After seventy-eight years of living there was no grieving husband, no children left behind. There was a brother, however, and a nephew and niece, and something else – a small, fat scrapbook, onto whose pages were lovingly written and stuck the history of a lifetime – and more, patiently collected, the history of a village in whose environs Miss Kidd, and her family before that even, had been irrefragably entwined.

Inherited from her mother, the wife of Edwin Kidd, coachman to Mrs J.W. Rowntree, widow of the late Quaker cocoa magnate, who resided in Scalby, and before that, in the employ of Lord Airedale of Cober Hill, Cloughton, and later, coachman to Mr James A. Cooke, proprietor of the *Hull News* and *Hull Daily*, the scrapbook was in turn started by her parents in the early to mid-nineteenth century.

The daughter of Mrs J.W. Rowntree, Miss Jean Rowntree, corresponded with, and visited 'Milly' Kidd, as she was popularly known to friends in Scalby, up until her end. In turn, and despite their differences, the spinster visited Miss Rowntree at her London home and elsewhere, often holidaying with her and the family too – they were lifetime friends

Manor House, Langdale End where Mrs J.W. Rowntree, widow of the 'Quaker Socialist', removed with her children from Scalby in 1924

Silhouette of John Cole and signature from his book
Historical Sketches of Scalby, Burniston & Cloughton,
published in 1829

and Miss Rowntree was familiar with the scrapbook, had even borrowed it, writing when she returned it, 'I have enjoyed reading the scrapbook – it is really your family scrapbook as well as your granny's', adding, 'I ought to post it back to you when I get back to the cottage[1] – you won't want to be without it . . .'.

How did I come by it, a total stranger?

I rescued it from a York postcard dealer some years back. Possibly on the death of Miss 'Milly' it had passed on to her surviving brother, Henry Francis Kidd, who died in 1986 and lived at Acomb, on the outskirts of York. Perhaps his children overlooked its importance during the sad and tiresome business of sorting his effects, discarding lightly a collection once so proudly cherished through three generations. Whatever the reason, the important fact is that through the Kidd family we are able to put together a picture of Scalby during its most glorious years, when the village flourished as the 'genteel suburb' of Scarborough and attracted a number of eminent men and women of the day; persons of the calibre of John W. Rowntree; Tom Laughton, whose family and later himself, owned a prestigious hotel in Scarborough, and who was brother of the actor, Charles Laughton; the Sitwells; and Will Catlin and his famous 'pierrot' family to name but a few who lived here and left their indelible stamp on this oft-praised community.

---

1.   Miss Jean Rowntree kept, and still keeps, a cottage at Home Farm, Brandsby, near Hovingham (NY).

CHAPTER ONE

The Early Years

John Cole described the village of Scalby as 'seated in a vale, surrounded by ranges of majestic hills, in the wapentake of Pickering-Lythe, in the North Riding of the county of York, distant from Scarborough 3 miles, 40 from York, 18 respectively from Pickering and Whitby, and from London *via* York, 237, *via* Lincoln, 211'. He went on to say, 'the situation of Scalby is more pleasant, and its general appearance more inviting, than many other villages of the county; it being agreeably dispersed; not having too much of the straight line, but presenting many rural deviations, both as regards the buildings themselves and their situation'. Unfortunately, Cole went on to somewhat detract from his glowing description by concluding, 'Scalby is what Leland would call, "a praty [pretty] thoroughfare" for Hackness.'[1]

The Victoria County History records that Scalby parish was composed in 1831 of the townships of Burniston, Cloughton, Newby, Scalby, Staintondale and Throxenby. The area of this parish was given as 11,759 acres of land, 380 acres of foreshore and 18 acres

Looking along North Street, into South Street, Scalby. The Temperance Hall stands on the corner (left) with 'Sedmans Butchers' in the foreground. Opposite on the right is the Nag's Head public house, under the ownership then of Tom Laughton. Tom Laughton was the brother of the actor Charles Laughton, and lived in Scalby village at one time, as did his other brother, Frank

of inland water.[2] In 1890 the parish comprised of townships of Scalby and Throxenby, the new area of the whole being 3,992 acres, and the population numbering 802; of this, the township of Scalby itself contained 2,730 acres (including 126 acres of sea coast) and held 600 inhabitants,[3] a figure unchanged from 1857[4] and 1859,[5] but which had risen steadily from 446 in 1823,[6] to 583 in 1840.[7]

Scalby is a place of considerable antiquity. In 1843 a tumulus in the vicinity, near to the large hill variously named Cambouts, Camboots or Cam Butts, was opened in which were found two urns with arrowheads of flint, and some bones. In Scarborough museum, where these relics were deposited, is also an ancient pitcher, found in Scalby churchyard, and on the estate of Mr Hardcastle, in 'Duck Field', Mr Manson, a tenant farmer, found a girdle of pure gold, 35 in long, weighing 2½ ounces. Afterward, on the marriage of Mr Hardcastle, this girdle formed part of the bride's adornments. All these are of prehistoric origin.

In the Domesday Book of *c.* 1086, Scalby formed part of the king's manor of Falsgrave,[8] and continued in the hands of the Crown until 1267,[9] when Henry II granted the manor to his son Edmund,[10] who in the same year received the honour of Pickering.[11] For some time afterward, Scalby was not accounted a part of that honour,[12] but became so by 1316.[13] The lands of Scalby subsequently came into the Percy family through William de Percy. Later on, Scalby became the lordship of Henry, Duke of Lancaster, who dying in 1362, caused his great estates to be divided between his two daughters, Maude and Blanche, the latter of whom was married to John of Gaunt, Earl of Richmond, afterward Duke of Lancaster. Today the manor still belongs to the Duchy of Lancaster.[14]

Scalby in the twelfth and thirteenth centuries was a Royal Forest and nearly all woodland. In 1086 the wood of Falsgrave, of which Scalby formed a part, measured three *leagues* long by two wide.[15] Between 1154 and 1162, however, Falsgrave declined in importance, while Scalby forest, no doubt composed of wooded lands between the River Derwent and the sea, had come into existence in its own right.[16] The Bolebec family held the bailiwick of the hay and forest of Scalby by hereditary title[17] until Osbert de Bolebec surrendered it at some time between 1252 and 1256 to the king, by whom it was granted at the latter date, to Hugh le Bigod.[18] The manor, like that of Pickering, was granted to Edmund, the king's son, and the Earl Marshal subsequently paid 63s. 4d. rent to the lord of Pickering for his bailiwick.[19] It is possible that for this reason, Scalby, being a separate manorial estate, was not accounted for as part of the honour of Pickering mentioned previously. Earl Edmund temporarily seized the bailwick on account of forest offences committed by Roger le Bigod and his servants,[20] and it was still in his possession in 1297.[21] In 1322 and afterward Scalby forest is referred to as the East Ward of Pickering Forest,[22] but in 1651 it was held that the manor of Scalby had never been in that forest, of which the River Derwent was the eastern boundary.[23]

It was during this period, toward the latter end of the thirteenth century, that Cole notes a controversy over land and grazing rights hereabouts. The dispute was between Thomas, prior of Bridlington, and Roger, abbot of Whitby, whereby in

1231, it was agreed that the prior should renounce all claim to common right of pasturage in Hackness, *Silshou*, and *Suthfield*, belonging to his freehold of Scalby, Burniston, and Cloughton; the abbot granting that the prior should have the right of pasture in Hayburn for 50 cows and their young under three years, and the liberty to grass 20 brood mares, with their foals until three years old, the prior paying annually, at Whitby, 1 lb of wax and 1 lb of incense. The abbot at the same time reserved the right of enclosing 500 acres of land within the above-named places, but in such manner as to allow free ingress and egress for the prior's cattle to and from the pasture of Hayburn.[24]

Undoubtedly, this passage was on the trackway which led south over the moors beginning at the Green Dyke and crossed the waters at Hayburn Beck Bridge, the point of entry, later confirmed in the Inclosure Award of 1829.

Green Dyke was an important boundary line at least as long as recorded history, and marked the divide between the wapentakes of Pickering-Lythe and Whitby Strand; between the Royal Forest of Scalby (later Pickering) and the forest of the abbot of Whitby, as well as between the townships of Staintondale (part of the old parish of Scalby) and Fylingdale. The name 'Green Dyke' occurs frequently in the early records of the Duchy of Lancaster and those of Whitby Abbey.[25]

By contrast, the first known reference to Hayburn Beck Bridge occurs in the survey of the boundaries of Scalby in 1621,[26] showing that, by the seventeenth century, it was the principal crossing of the beck, although there are signs of another and older road through Staintondale, running nearer and roughly parallel to the cliffs. There are also traces of this older thoroughfare in Cloughton, south of Hayburn Wyke Hotel, where it runs alongside the old railway line.[27]

Another contest, between the canons of Bridlington Priory and the Cistercian monks of Scarborough, was resolved in 1281, when it was determined that the canons should have half the tithe of such animals belonging to the parish of Scarborough as were fed in the parish of Scalby, or in proportion to the time they might be pastured there.[28]

King Henry II gave free pasture to his forest at this place, for all the swine belonging to the Bridlington canons, at the time when other hogs fed in the said forest.[29]

The original purpose of the forest enclosures with their carefully guarded Forest Laws, was the protection of the king's beasts and of the woodlands in which they dwelled, and to provide secondary, and later, a source of, revenue.

With vast areas of the neighbourhood covered by forest, the early inhabitants of Scalby, in common with the rest of the country, would use wood for fuel or charcoal made from wood. However, when the Forest Law was applied to the area with the coming of the Norman lords, a great and almost punitive limitation of supply took place. The forest authorities insisted on the conservation of the woodlands to protect the domain of the deer.

Within the forest no resident was allowed to cut down a tree, even on his own land, without permission, unless he was able to prove, as some of the lords did, that for one reason or another the Forest Law did not apply to his property – a legal argument not likely to be available to the peasantry of Scalby!

It is not surprising, therefore, that innumerable cases of illegal tree felling were brought before the Forest Justice,[30] the offenders varying from such magnates as the priors of Malton and Bridlington down to the humblest cottager. Some of the numbers of trees unlawfully felled are outrageous – the Constable of Pickering Castle, himself the nominal head of the forest, was asked to explain (which he was quite unable to do satisfactorily) to the Forest Assize of 1335, the felling of over six hundred oak trees from Scalby Hay and elsewhere.[31]

Frequently the forest villages were indicted for 'wasting' or spoiling their local woodlands by the unauthorized taking of timber when the foresters were engaged elsewhere. In these instances, the Forest Law would be invoked and the area concerned taken back into the king's ownership and only released on the payment of a heavy fine. This happened to the woods in nearby Staintondale in 1335.[32]

Interestingly, the record of this offence is one of many recorded in the great Pickering Forest Eyre or Assize, commenced in the previous year on Monday 6 October, nominally held at Pickering. The visit was a belated one; an earlier forest court at Pickering appears to have been held in 1288,[33] at a time when Edward I had granted to his brother, Edmund Crouchback, Earl of Lancaster, the services of the Royal Forest Justices and with it, the privilege of retaining all the fines and profits from the Assize (a very large sum indeed) which normally would have gone into the king's coffers!

The presiding Justice at the 1334 Assize at Pickering was Richard de Willoughby, a surprising choice then, considering his record of corruption.[34] The Justices sat not only at Pickering, but also at times at Hackness, within the forest of the abbot of Whitby so that offences committed in that area could be dealt with during their visit.

The Assize lasted some years, at least until 1338, for there was an enormous backlog of offenders to deal with, many in fact who had died in the meantime! In most cases the Pickering *Coucher Book*, which contains details of the affair, does not give the date of an offence, but occasionally this is recorded and from these one can see that some offences go back as far as 1292 – some forty-two years previous! If the court found that the accused man had died then his son, or failing that, his surety, was fined in his place. Only with the greatest reluctance was a case dropped, so lucrative and important was the income generated by this Forest Eyre.

The first act the president of the court did, was to summon to Pickering all the free tenants within the forest, together with the Reeve (steward) and four men from each township to hear the proposed programme for the Assize. Absentees were substantially fined, and few excuses were tolerated.

The hundreds of defendants and witnesses, alongside the huge numbers of forest officials, meant an incredible amount of administration, much of which was diligently recorded. In one instance a case of poaching was mentioned under the day Tuesday 10 July 1311:

> Robert, son of John Scalby; John lad of William Nafferton, vicar of Scalby and William Capel . . . carried to the vicar's house, with out his knowledge, a hind which Robert had killed, there skinned it. Dionysia, the vicar's maid, was an accessory, and had part of the venison, the other part she sent as a gift to Emma Pinchon, laundress of Newby and to the vicar's ploughman for their dinner, when they went ploughing for the vicar. William Capel fined 6s and 8d; the rest outlawed.

Justice was rough and above all speedy. The system appears to have been to fine the offender according to his ability to pay, and if he had no money or means of paying the fine, he was outlawed, often for the most trivial of reasons. The *Coucher Book* gives a list of over two hundred names of men accused of 'hunting the hare within the forest' – a very mild offence. The clerk who recorded the list concludes with the remark, 'some appear and are fined, some do not appear and are outlawed and some are dead'.[35]

Despite stringently imposed Forest Laws, within the bounds of such Royal enclosures, the right of freewarren – to 'hunt with dogs' – was often bestowed by the king on monastic houses and on favoured individuals and lords. It was always understood, however, to strictly exclude the taking of deer and wild boar, both of which were considered to be 'royal' beasts.

Normally all dogs in the forest had to be 'lawed' – that is, to have three claws on each forefoot struck off to make the animal, in theory at least, useless for hunting.[36] However, the records show that the order was widely disregarded. In 1327 an official enquiry found that there were 135 unlawed dogs within the forest of Pickering – little wonder there was so much poaching![37] The prior of Bridlington, whose land overlapped that of the Knights Hospitallers at Hayburn, was brought before the Forest Justices in 1334 for having unlawed dogs in the parish of Scalby. He invoked, with success, a grant of king Stephen and also the Magna Carta to prove that the priory had exemption from the 'lawing' of dogs.[38]

A detailed account of the privilege of freewarren is given in the Pickering records[39] where an entry in the *Coucher Book* reads,

Know ye that we [Henry III] have granted to our beloved burgess, Robert Hardy of Scarborough, that during his life-time he may enjoy the liberty of hunting with his hounds the hare, fox, wild-cat and badger throughout the Forest of Pickering, except during the 'fence' month, without let or hinderance from any officer of the forest. Nevertheless, he shall take none of our deer under cover of this grant: given at Canterbury, June 1253.

The 'fence' month was from two weeks before Midsummer Day to two weeks after; this was the time the hinds were fauning. As the taking of the wild boar was not expressly forbidden in the grant, it may be assumed that the animal no longer existed in the forest of Scalby at this period, though some years later the same king dispatched two of his hunters (one of whom rejoiced in the name of 'John the Fool') to Pickering Forest to take 'twenty hinds and ten pigs [wild boar]' for the royal larder.[40]

Although the right of hunting with dogs was often passed on, there can be little possibility of any such continuity between these early grants and the present-day nearby Staintondale Hunt. Indeed, it would seem certain that the firmly held religious beliefs of the Quakers, so strong on the ground hereabouts during the sixteenth to eighteenth centuries, would cause them to look sourly at what they would doubtless consider the frivolous sport of foxhunting and take pains to stamp it out during these years!

NOTES

1. Cole, John, *Historical Sketches of Scalby, Burniston & Cloughton*, 1829.
2. VCH.NR(i) 1914.
3. Bulmer's *History & Directory of North Yorkshire*, 1890.
4. Kelly's *Post Office Directory*, 1857.
5. Whellan & Co., *North Riding of Yorkshire Directory*, 1859.
6. Baines' *Yorkshire Directory* (Vol. II North & East Riding), 1823.
7. White's *Yorkshire Directory*, 1840.

8. VCH.NR(ii) 1923.
9. *Pipe. R.* 15 Hen. II (Pipe Roll Soc.), 37; *Pipe. R.* Hen. II, m.1d; 2 Rich. I, m.7; 8 Rich. I, m.16; 4 John, m.4; 8 John, m.20; 16 John, m.8; *Cal. Rot. Chart.* 1199–1216 (Rec. Com.), 85b; *Hun. R.* (Rec. Com.), i, 108.
10. Duchy of Lancaster Misc. Bks. xi, 62d.
11. Ibid.
12. *Cal. Pat.* 1281–1292, p. 477; *Yorks. Inq.* (YAS), iii, p. 74; *Hund. R.* (Rec. Com.), i, 108.
13. *Kirby's Inq.* (Surt. Soc.), 327.
14. Bulmer's, op. cit., 1890.
15. VCH.NR(ii) 1923.
16. Duchy of Lanc. Royal Chart. Gt. Coucher, i, f. 3786; *Pipe. R.* (Pipe Roll Soc.) 14 Hen. II, 90–91.
17. *Excerpta e Rot.Fin.* (Rec. Com), ii, 144.
18. *Pipe. R.* 2 John, m.12d; *Red Bk. Exch.* (Rolls Ser.) pp. lxxv–vi.
19. *Yorks.Inq.* (YAS), iii, 74.
20. *Hon . . . Pickering*, ii, 35–45, where there is given a list of the Earl Marshal's offences and the profits of his bailiwick; cf. *ibid.* iii, 232.
21. *Yorks. Inq.* (YAS), iii, 73–74.
22. *Hon . . . Pickering*, i, p. xix; iv, p. 200.
23. Ibid. i, p. 94.
24. Cole, op. cit.
25. Rimmington, F.C., *The History of Ravenscar & Staintondale*, Scarboro' Arch. & Hist. Soc., 1988.
26. Turton, R.B. (ed.), *The Honour & Forest of Pickering*, NRRS, New Ser. Vol. I., p. 21, 1894.
27. Rimmington, op. cit.
28. Cole, op. cit.
29. Ibid.
30. Turton, R.B. (ed.), *The Honour & Forest of Pickering*. NRRS, New Ser. Vols. I–IV, 1894–97, iii. p. 44.
31. Ibid., ii, p. 130.
32. Ibid., iv, p. 37.
33. Ibid., iv, p. 12.
34. Ibid., ii, p. 34.
35. Ibid., iii, p. 44.
36. Ibid., iv, p. 18.
37. Ibid., iv, p. 19.
38. Ibid., iii, p. 6.
39. Ibid., ii, p. 121.
40. Ibid., ii, p. 219.

CHAPTER TWO

Of Bricks and Mortar

According to the Victoria County History, Scalby possessed a manorial hall in the twelfth century,[1] and it is said that there was a Guildhall, destroyed by fire around the time of James I. No description survives, but the site of the former was probably that on which the present Scalby Hall stands. The Hall was rebuilt in the style of the day and dates from the late eighteenth century, but it is possible that another hall may have been erected between the two dates.

The front elevation presents an imposing façade, and is constructed of a uniform grey ashlar, quite unlike the warmer coloured local hardstone and freestone which was quarried up until this century at nearby Cloughton. By contrast, however, the rear of Scalby Hall is formed of common brick. The gardens, it is said, were extensive, and sloped gently down to the 'Cut' and as the Hall stood well back at the highest point, visitors and those passing by always saw its most presentable aspect.

The approach was made by a long, sweeping drive between an avenue of beech trees, and the entrance to the Hall was marked by a small but picturesque gatehouse in the

Church Beck House, Scalby, showing the later extension of 1906

The eighteenth-century garden 'belvedere', all that
is left of the original Low Hall, which was pulled
down and subsequently rebuilt for John W.
Rowntree

'gothick' style which still remains, though somewhat hidden away beside the Newby
bridge on the main Scarborough to Whitby highway.

It was here, at Scalby Hall, that Timothy Hardcastle lived just over a century ago. He
was reputed to be the last of the constables chosen before Sir Robert Peel introduced the
regular police force. The Court Leet appointed constables from Scalby and Newby
alternately, each serving a term of two years. During the term of a Newby officer, the
following 'doggerel' was often heard around the neighbourhood:

> When the constable goes up the Newby Hill
> Then beware the HUNGILL.

This *Hungill* or *Hungelt* appears to have been a small, local tax of sorts, probably a
relic of the old Forest Law, which applied only to Scalby township. When the constable
was of that village, he would no doubt feel as unwilling to collect this tax as the
villagers were to pay it. But the Newby men, possibly slightly jealous of their larger and
richer neighbour, would have no such qualms, and would scrupulously enforce it –
hence the couplet.

Preceding the Hardcastle family, who had moved into Church Beck House by 1905[2]
(although the widow of Timothy, Mrs Betsy Hardcastle, is recorded as living at Scalby
Villa in 1890,[3]) the Hall was lived in by one Richard Rudgard. He was resident there in

1890[4] and still *in situ* in 1905.[5] Earlier in 1872, Scalby Hall was given as the address of Robert Green, often referred to as 'Squire Green'.

Today, like many old halls and mansions, the building, deemed too large for a family house, is converted into flats, but still retains a little of its former splendour in its ornamental gardens and a few ancient trees.

Scalby Low Hall, was said to have been a fine red-brick residence in Church Becks, dating from the seventeenth century. All that now remains of this, is a small, square sandstone ashlar belvedere or summer house of *c.* 1750 in what was the kitchen garden to the 'new' Low Hall. At one time there was a shallow arch beneath this, from which, legend has it, an underground passage connected with the old Low Hall.

The present Low Hall which takes its name from the former, but not the site, was designed by Frederick Rowntree (1860–1927), the London architect, for John Wilhelm Rowntree and erected in 1904. J.W. Rowntree was the cocoa manufacturer of York, and a prominent member of the Society of Friends (Quakers). He was referred to as the 'prophet of the renaissance' of Quakerism towards the end of the nineteenth century when a 'new spiritual fervour in alliance with modern thought spread through the Society of Friends'. Unfortunately, by this time, J.W. Rowntree was an invalid, planning to retire to Scalby to work mainly on his research for a history of Quakerism, and to devote his time to Adult School Education, and for which he had the upper floor of Low Hall designed to accommodate guests attending schools in the neighbourhood. Sadly J.W. Rowntree never lived there, he died on a trip to America before he could take up residence. His widow and children remained for some years before moving in 1924 to the Manor House at Langdale

Low Hall Cottage, 1906: part of J.W. Rowntree's rebuilding of Low Hall. The cottage provided staff accommodation and is one of a pair standing opposite each other

Yew Court, Scalby. The gate piers built *c.* 1742 at
a cost of £60 – considered then 'a simple entrance'

End, when Low Hall subsequently became a miners' convalescent home. It was during the period when Mrs J.W. Rowntree was *in situ*, that Milly Kidd's parents were employed at Low Hall.

Probably the most notable building in the village is Yew Court, built in 1742 for a Captain Ians. John Cole refers to it thus:

> at the eastern end of the village is an irregular building, presenting an angular projection at the east end, and with gardens of the old style of decoration, with yew-trees, cut into fantastic shapes, and in general suited to the appearance of the house, which is grotesque and singular.[6]

Yew Court replaced an earlier residence thought to be of ecclesiastical origins, which over the years has given rise to a great deal of folklore hereabouts.

By 1761 the house had been sold on, and was in the hands of Ralph Betsons, Town Clerk of Scarborough, who in that year entertained the then Duke of York to a meal at Yew Court when His Highness was presented with the Freedom of the Borough on 15 August – an event about which one local historian, Mr J.D. Tickle once remarked, 'and much has been made of this very ordinary occurrence ever since'.[7]

The old part of the building facing High Street has not altered greatly through the years – including the distinctive circular gate piers of dressed sandstone which incorporate garden rooms and which formed the 'simple entrance' to Yew Court and cost the sum of £60, considered expensive in 1742, about the time of their construction. From 1895 onward, however, substantial extensions were made to the Scalby Road elevation, when Mr W. Tingle Brown occupied the house. It was he who added the numerous gables, extending it from a single bay to five in length.

The artist, Atkinson Grimshaw, was familiar with Yew Court. In 1874, before alterations, he painted, *The Old Gate; Yew Court, Scalby* (oil on paper on panel, 17.8 x 43.2 cm [7 x 17 in]) for Thomas Jarvis, a wealthy Scarborough brewer. Three years later he returned to paint a garden scene with a young girl admiring the flowers – lilies, Grimshaw's favourite bloom. His picture was entitled, *The Rector's Garden: Queen of the Lilies* (oil on canvas, 80 x 122 cm [13½ x 48 in]. Preston, Harris Museum & Art Gallery). The figure herself may have been a member of the then owner's family, but a certain stiffness implies that her elegance may owe more to a fashion-plate engraving than to actual observation.[8]

Following Ralph Betson as owner of Yew Court in the late eighteenth century, was one John Parkin – known as 'Squire Parkin'. Scalby village did not always have a squire. In

Traditionally a monastic foundation, Yew Court, Scalby, drawn for the Mercury by Raymond Fieldhouse was reconstructed in 1742. In 1761 it was the property of Ralph Betson, Town Clerk of Scarborough, who entertained there Prince Edward Augustus, Duke of York and Albany, the younger brother of King George III

the Middle Ages, King John, often in need of revenue, leased off the manor house and manorial lands for a period to a consortium of tenants from the village, who managed the affairs of the estate through a bailiff's court of their own. Nevertheless, there was usually someone who played the role, more often than not, the resident of Scalby Hall.

Throughout this period it was the de Barughs and the Goldsbroughs, later the Hinderwell and Keld families. By the eighteenth century, however, events had moved on, and Scalby had already begun to adopt the trappings of a genteel suburb for the more prosperous in flight from 'town life' in Scarborough. Prominent townsmen – Mayor Knowsley, Plaxton Dickinson and the Bell family of 14 St Nicholas Street – all had a residence in the village, often modernizing a cottage or farmstead for their families' use.

John Parkin – 'Squire Parkin' – was another. His ancestors had lived in St Mary's Quarter, Scarborough, and were already reckoned 'genteel' in 1702. Their older, medieval house, which gave its name to Parkin Lane in Quay Street, Scarborough, had itself been a fine dwelling by the standards of an earlier day.

A relative had acquired a farmstead at Scalby from the Knowsley family early in the eighteenth century, and he sold it to his relative, George Parkin, of Scarborough. It was on the south side of the main street (High Street) to the east of Keld's hospital cottages. Later in the century the Parkins also tenanted Yew Court. To one or the other of these buildings John Parkin took his family each summer.

Parkin was a sailmaker, a prosperous occupation in the days of wooden sailing ships, when Scarborough's sea front was not a line of parked cars but of moored boats. Shipbuilding was the port's real trade and summer visitors were curiosities, a mere accessory chiefly dealt with in the upper area of the town around Queen Street, St Nicholas Street and Newborough. The visitor's coast stretched from the valley approaches to the Spaw-house and beyond – a genteel world of the Assembly, Coffee-House and Spaw – and the Scalby 'squire', among many, took on something of this new elegance of the age, separating the two world's of commerce and leisure.

From his summer residence in the village he rode his 'Yarmouth Cart' into town, with 'John Parkin, Esquire' carefully inscribed on the side; he avoided Nonconformity and attended the Church of England; his daughters learnt their manners at private academies. Thus, John Parkin qualified himself for civic office and became, in time, one of the 'Forty-four', the inner circle of freemen who had the vote in Georgian Scarborough, whether for a member of Parliament or in forming the local government body of the time. Unfortunately, it was Parkin's ambition in the arena of politics that in 1788 led to his subsequent fall from grace, when he set himself up to become one of the two bailiffs at the annual election at the Common Hall on St Jerome's Day. After dining at the Golden Hall Inn, the voters were locked in together until a decision was reached.

The voting procedure was a complicated one, but its purpose simpler. It enabled a series of co-options to take place among the 'Forty-four', so that the bailiffs were sure of a body of connected support in the first twelve, or in modern terms, the 'Council', and among the officers serving it. The vote gave its premiums to the well-connected and the well-organized, often resulting in a group of close friends and relatives controlling the corporation. Sadly John Parkin proved insufficiently well-connected or well-organized as the following verses penned at the time show:

The Scalby Squire of high renown,
This morning came from that fair town,
Apparel'd in his best array,
In honour of the happy day,
When he should shine in Bailiffs gown
And on the vulgar proudly frown.

His body decked with care and art,
He scorned to ride in Yarmouth Cart
So trudged along with stick in hand,
Upheld, and fancying it a wand,
And as he mark'd the dreary way,
Thus to himself was heard to say.

When I'm locked up as now I must
I'll in the house kick up a dust,
Myself I will a bailiff make,
And for my daughter Tompy's sake
Robson my son shall Town Clerk be
Then who so great as he and me?

My breeches are of strongest kind
And for this purpose doubly lined.
So I can sit out every man
Who dares oppose my deep laid plan.
And thus I'll bring the dogs to reason,
For now or never is the season.

Despite his confidence, 'Squire Parkin's' schemes for securing votes became known to the opposition, and Mr William Clarkson, a butcher (and the then bailiff), and John Travis, a town surgeon, mustered their forces, and when the 'Forty-four' assembled in the Common Hall, quickly nominated a Mr Haggett and Mr Hopper as referees instead of Parkin's cousin John, as had been planned. Mr James Tindall and Mr W. Duesbury were then speedily named bailiffs and it was all over for 'Squire Parkin', who in conclusion was heard to say:

G—d—n the Butcher, curse the day,
When all my plans for self and son
Are by his malice quite undone.

After 'Squire Parkin', the ownership of Yew Court came into the hands of his daughters; Cole records it as being in their possession by 1829, noting that it was 'the summer residence of the Misses Parkin, of Scarborough'.[9] It may be inferred from this statement that, by the early nineteenth century, Yew Court was somehow divided up into separate residences and partly let off, as it is known that the Abram family lived here at this period, into whom the Kidd family married in the nineteenth century. By that date,

The nineteenth-century stable-block erected by local mason, John Robinson, to serve Yew Court. Notice the considerable number of pigeon holes which would house pigeons to provide 'game' for the pigeon pie! The stables have been converted into a house

however, the Abram family, their circumstances reduced by bad investment, had moved to nearby Burniston, where John Abram and his wife still remained a respected pillar of the community and lived comfortably at Cockrah Farm.

Later occupants of Yew Court include Mr & Mrs Spencer, of Marks & Spencer fame, and the Catlins, a renowned 'pierrot' family, who left a legacy in Scarborough that has endured to this day. It is not known when Will Catlin first lived at Yew Court, but he first appeared at Scarborough in 1894. At this time Will formed a troupe who entertained on the sands. The following year he was engaged to appear at the Aquarium, which was known then as the People's Palace Music Hall, under the direction of William Morgan. Will also appeared at the opening performance at the People's Palace in Bridlington that year.

In 1896 he was back on the sands at Scarborough, and having spent a previous year in partnership, he negotiated to take over the entire show.

This was a step which was to influence the course of his life. His name was to become irrevocably linked with seaside entertainment and Scarborough. From a comparatively unknown performer he was to become one of the greatest pioneers of seaside entertainment in all its forms.[10]

Catlin dressed his troupe in pierrot costumes consisting of black skull caps surmounted by a white conical hat, white suit with ruffles at the neck and wrists and

Yew Court, Scalby today. Taken from the main Scarborough–Whitby Road showing the original parts and later rebuildings behind

Will Catlin (back centre) and his troupe of pierrots in 1908. Catlin lived at Yew Court for a number of years

black pom poms. This garb was to become familiar to the seaside going public in later years, but in the 1890s was something of a novelty.[11]

Will's brother Tom, sometimes referred to as Tom Braham-Fox, soon joined him in his venture, and they ran two troupes simultaneously, Will on the South Beach opposite the Aquarium, and Tom's 'Red Pom Poms' at the North Bay. Eventually Will Catlin had troupes under his direction performing in numerous principal seaside resorts as far apart as Bournemouth and Whitley Bay.[12]

Catlin's rival at that time was Tom Carrick, already established in Scarborough when Will arrived in the town. Each vied for the prime pitches on the beach which were auctioned by the Corporation every season.

In 1906, Will cleverly secured all the pitches forcing his rivals to move on to other venues. The original 'rent' charged by the Corporation was still then 'a bob a nob' per day for each performer. This was six shillings [30p] per week per man, and amounted to a collective sum of five to six pounds per week.[13]

The Catlin pierrot troupes were in the early years all male shows. It was not until the advent of the First World War and with it the subsequent shortage of male performers, which caused him, reluctantly, to engage female entertainers. It has been suggested that Will's aversion to women performers was possibly due to the fact that he had a family of one son and six daughters whom he openly discouraged from entering the profession. He forbade his children to marry into 'the business' but in spite of this, two of his daughters, Gladys and Topsy, did eventually marry pierrots.[14]

The troupe gave three performances a day when the weather was fine. Only severe inclement weather or exceptionally high tides prevented them from entertaining. The money was collected from the people who paid for the deck-chairs set out in front of the stage, and also by 'bottling' – passing a bag on the end of a stick amongst the people standing on the wall or around the stage.[15]

In the first year, Will's show on the beach made a modest profit, but as its popularity increased, so did the demands of the Corporation for the rent of the pitches.[16]

By 1903, they were demanding £650 and by 1908 the demands had become unreasonable, and they were said to exceed four figures. Will's reaction to this situation was a flat refusal to pay. The councillors were mortified, but Catlin, not to be dismayed, moved the whole company to a new site near the Grand Hotel. The

THE HULL TIMES, JULY 21, 1900—7

"HULL TIMES" WEEKLY CARTOON.

A topical cartoon of pierrots performing at the seaside

Council retaliated by declaring this unsafe so Catlin with his usual business acumen responded by buying some land where the present Futurist Theatre now stands, and erected a covered wooden alfresco for the shows. This was to become the first Arcadia Theatre.[17]

The Arcadia Theatre quickly established itself, and the Catlin's were soon playing to audiences of two thousand seated and as many standing. It is said that in the course of his career, Will Catlin made somewhere in the region of twenty thousand personal appearances at Scarborough alone!

Will further extended his interests by acquiring the rights to the kiosk on Clarence Gardens. Due to the short-sighted policy of the Council, the Corporation lost a lucrative contract. The Arcadia was the beginning of the foreshore developments that are synonymous with the name of Catlin.

Up to this time Will had lived in Leicester, but in 1910, he moved to Scarborough and took up permanent residence. He began a development programme which included the Arcadia Restaurant, the Palladium Cinema and the acquired Olympia.[18]

In 1913 Catlin began an ambitious scheme – the Kingscliffe Holiday Camp – which included a dining-room capable of seating 520 people and a handsome concert hall with seating for 900 people. Sleeping and living facilities were intended to accommodate 1,000 people. He further endeared himself to the local population by employing only Scarborough men to do the work. A local contractor directed the work and a local architect prepared the plans.[19]

Sadly, a year later, Will suffered a double blow with the onset of hostilities with Germany. First, the holiday season was cut short when the excursion trains were discontinued to be used for the movement of troops and equipment. Second, one of the first shells to land on Scarborough is said to have destroyed the show's entire wardrobe at Clarence Gardens, and damage was also caused at his Kingscliffe Camp.[20]

One could be forgiven for assuming that the middle-aged Will would have rested on his laurels, having enjoyed so much success and adulation in his chosen profession. From modest beginnings he had performed before, and had been presented to, Royalty, including Edward VII and the Prince of Wales later to become King George V. He had turned down opportunities to perform on the London stage with staggering fees being offered and had become a man of property.[21]

Will never even considered retirement; for a short time the family moved back to Leicester, but were soon back in Scarborough. There were now Catlin shows in resorts too numerous to mention. He had always had a particular liking for the Welsh resort Llandudno, and it was here Will Catlin chose to live out his later years. He never did retire, and was constantly to be seen at one or other of his theatres, taking a personal interest in the presentation of all his shows.[22]

Two weeks before his death he made what was to be his last visit to Scarborough to see for himself the current show. His humorous and disheartening experiences

CATLIN'S
ROYAL PIERROTS

GIVE ENTERTAINMENTS DAILY
During the Summer Season, at the following places :—

Arcadia, Scarboro.
MANAGER, MR. W. CATLIN.

Arcadia, Colwyn Bay.
MANAGER, MR. SID FRERE.

Beach Pavilion, Bournemouth
MANAGER, MR. G. HOUGHTON.

Beach Pavilion, Bournemouth
MANAGER, MR. H. LOVELL.

Assembly Rooms, Withernsea.
MANAGER, MR. C. MILNER.

Park Pavilion, Erith.
MANAGER, MR. F. BLYTHE.

Wellington Pier, Yarmouth.
MANAGER, MR. T. BRAHAM FOX.

A playbill showing the number and extent of Will Catlin's troupes of pierrots

made him a very understanding 'guvnor'. Never at any time did he ask one of his troupe to do anything he was not prepared to do himself. This was largely the key to his phenomenal success as it inspired confidence and support, coupled with his astute business acumen which motivated him to purchase one of the finest sites in Scarborough at the right time, and to make films of current events, including members of his troupe, thus putting the Catlins among the first of the British film actors.[23]

Catlin was advised to retire on more than one occasion, but the advice fell on deaf ears. On the 15th January 1953, Will left his home in Llandudno with the object of seeing his show at the Arcadia Theatre. He was to have attended the rehearsal of Catlin's Follies, but he collapsed and died in his car outside the theatre at the age of eighty-five. In true Catlin tradition the show went on that evening and the audience was not given the sad news until the end of the performance.[24]

Will Catlin was born William Henry Fox in Leicester in 1871. His father, a publican, was the landlord of the King William IV in Colton Street, and he was also a county cricketer of some distinction.

Young Will was educated at the British Boys' School, and in due course was apprenticed to a tailor's cutter. This was not entirely to his liking and it was very soon obvious that he had no intention of staying in such a mundane occupation, although the little experience he gained was to prove most useful at a later date when he designed and sewed the troupes' original costumes. He had been interested in the stage from a very early age, and as an adolescent Will became a familiar figure on the concert platforms around Leicester. He had a flair for entertainment and rapidly established a reputation as a polished amateur performer.

At the age of nineteen, undeterred by the fickleness of public taste and all the hazards of earning one's living 'on the boards', Will abandoned the occupation which did not appeal to him in favour of a professional career as an entertainer, producer and proprietor. Perhaps, it may be argued, he was more fortunate than some, but nearer the truth is the fact that Will always made the most of every chance, and was never afraid of hard work. His first professional venture was with a young man called Charlie Carson (later Danton) as a double act on the music-hall stage. It was at this juncture that he changed his name to Catlin – simply deciding that the double billing as Catlin and Carson was preferable to Fox and Carson. Together they worked the Moss Stoll Syndicate and appeared in various parts of the country.

It could be said that Will Catlin was a big man in all senses of the word. He was tall, broad shouldered, and was said by those who knew him to have had an inspiring presence. It would be fair to say that he took the last exit in a way that if given a choice, he would have chosen for himself. A conical pierrot hat made from white flowers rested on his coffin, bearing a card which read, 'King of the Pierrots final curtain, with deepest respect from 1953 Catlin's Follies'. Surely a fitting tribute to a remarkable showman.

Other dwellings of note in Scalby include 'The Holt' opposite Yew Court. Despite its somewhat eccentric appearance, this range of buildings was only built in 1882, for Thomas Cooke, one of the foremost telescope-makers of the nineteenth century[25] as the monogram and date testify. A sumptuous dwelling, it is built in the 'Domestic Revival'

The Holt, Scalby, where Henry Kidd and his wife were 'in service' to Mr J.A. Cooke, proprietor of *The Hull Daily News*

style of architecture and incorporates overhanging bracketed eaves and timber-framed jettied gables, all of which are richly carved with foliage and fruit, and finished with finials and the whole is surmounted with a steeply pitched, irregular roof and chimney stacks.

Internally, only the part known as 'Scalby Holt' remains unchanged, and here we find the main drawing-room of the original house, with its ornate classical-style carved timber fireplace painted white and fluted Ionic pilasters and entablature. There are also enriched paired pilasters of the same order on tall panelled pedestals framing an alcove, and a deep, richly carved entablature running around the room.

From 1887 it was here that Edwin Kidd was coachman to Mr James A. Cooke, Thomas's son, and he and his wife Louisa lived at one time in the adjoining lodge – Holt Cottage.

Part of the 'Holt' occupies the site of a spring of chalybeate waters, often and confusingly referred to as the 'Spa', which spilt itself on to the road before it was culverted down Scalby Beck. It was at Scalby Holt that King Edward VII was believed to have entertained Lillie Langtree, the Edwardian music-hall star, on several occasions – her horse, it is said, was stabled further down the High Street in a block built in the same style as the main house, and which is now 'The Gatehouse' restaurant.

Ironically, it was Mr Cooke who had the first motor car in the village, and it is told that the gardener, Mike Hill, frequently had to push it up the small incline running from the

The Lodge to Scalby Manor, formerly 'Wyndyate', both of which were built in the nineteenth-century 'Queen Anne' style of architecture. Erected by Edwin Brough, the Lodge house carries the heraldic arms of the Brough family; Argent, on a saltire sable, five swans of the first. *Crest*. A swan's head and neck erased

'Cut' to the crossroads on Scalby Road. This consequently became known locally as Cooke's Hill.

Towards the extreme west of the village, and nestling almost out of sight in lands that extended from Hay Lane to Carr Lane, stands the property Hay Brow. This was for some time the home of Sir George Sitwell and his young family before their move to Wood End, Scarborough.

Another dwelling occupying a site on the extremity of Scalby is 'Wyndyate', now known as Scalby Manor Hotel, which was once the home of the eccentric Edwin Brough. Born in Leek, in Staffordshire, he moved to Somerset in 1882, but two years later he decided to move north, and came to Scalby where he purchased the site, and built the residence 'Wyndyate' for his new bride in red brick in the 'Queen Anne' style of architecture. He was a Justice of the Peace for the North Riding, but is more commonly remembered for his interest in bloodhounds. He kept a range of famous kennels, and two of his hounds – Burgho and Barnaby – became famous themselves on the streets of London when engaged in tracking 'Jack the Ripper' during the notorious nineteenth-century Whitechapel murders.

Edwin Brough sat on the committee of the Kennel Club, which holds the same position in matters canine as the Jockey Club does in racing affairs. A bright, genial man, his pack of man-hunting bloodhounds drew many visitors to 'Wyndyate', while today descendants of these hounds are still housed in the original kennels.

On the furthest reaches of Scalby, also, like Hay Brow, named from the rising land which it occupied, is Wrea Head (Rea Head on some maps), erected for Mr J.E. Ellis in 1881. He was Liberal member for Parliament, who held office under Gladstone. Ellis and his family lived here for eighty years, although two sons, one a scientist, died tragically early. A twin daughter married Lord Parmoor, the other went to prison for distributing pacifist pamphlets during the 1914 war. Throughout their lives Mr & Mrs Ellis did much to benefit the village. On his death Mr Ellis's widow lived on regally at Wrea Head. Following her death, the building became a college run by the North Yorkshire Education Committee. Today, like Scalby Manor above, it functions as a country house hotel.

A contemporary newspaper account in the Kidd family album records the unfortunate demise of a son of Mr Ellis in the following manner:

Further particulars have come to hand respecting the sad death of Mr Arthur Edward Ellis [b. Feb 7 1870 – d. May 31 1891], son of Mr J.E. Ellis, MP, whose death was briefly announced yesterday. It appears that the deceased had been subject to periodical fits of depression ever since the death of his brother in October, 1890, and had sought medical advice. Under his doctor's orders he left Cambridge for some four months last year, and the rest and change appeared to have had a beneficial effect upon his health and state of mind. Since October last, when he returned to Cambridge [University], he had been quite cheerful and appeared to be shaking off the fits of depression. On Saturday last he went for a walk with a friend and afterwards had tea with him, when he seemed to be in the best of spirits. He also

Wrea Head, formerly the home of the nineteenth-century Liberal MP, J.E. Ellis, who held office under Prime Minister Gladstone. Later, it was taken over as a college of education. Today it is a country house hotel

arranged to breakfast on Sunday morning with Mr Powell, another intimate friend. Not keeping his engagement, Mr Powell went to the deceased's room and knocking at the door walked straight in. He was horrified to see Mr Ellis lying in his bed, with a bullet wound in his right temple. Mr Powell went for assistance and a doctor. It was discovered that the deceased held a five-chambered revolver tightly grasped in his right hand, two chambers of which were loaded and three were empty. It was evident that the deceased had fired two shots, the first had struck and splintered the door of the bedroom, and the second shot had lodged in his head. Death must have been instantaneous and it was only too obvious from the position of the body and the revolver that the wound was self-inflicted. There can be no doubt, after hearing the evidence of Mr Ellis, the father, and that of Dr Verrall, the unfortunate gentleman's tutor, that the deceased's mind had been affected by the death of his brother, and after suffering from periodical fits of depression, he took his own life whilst suffering from temporary insanity.

Further residences of interest in the neighbourhood include Prospect House in Carr Lane, typical of the type of good-class farmhouse of the early nineteenth century. It was built in 1817 for Mr Williamson, a Quaker, who was always referred to henceforth as 'Quaker Williamson'. On his death, great interest was aroused in the village by the Quaker women who came to the house to pay their respects in traditional 'Quaker' attire. Although 'Quaker Williamson' left instructions to be buried in the garden of Prospect House, his remains were interred in the Friend's Burial Ground at Scarborough.

The next occupant of Prospect House was a local yeoman farmer by the name of Smithson, and because he came to live in the 'Quaker' house, he was ever afterwards known as 'Quaker Smithson' whatever his religious persuasion.

Elsewhere in the village, the old vicarage on North Street was originally a rather small house, with a thatched roof, dwarfed amid the tall surrounding elms which still exist. A new and much larger house was built in its place. Erected in 1781 of stone from Cloughton quarry,[26] it was once described as 'ornate and dignified in front, cheap and ugly behind'.[27] This suggests that it was built in the manner of Scalby Hall, with good ashlar-dressed stone to the main façade and brick used extensively at the rear. Eventually this was replaced by another vicarage, bought and presented to the church by the late Mrs W. Tingle Brown.

Another house with 'ecclesiastical' connections, is the Manse in Low Street. Of Georgian date with early nineteenth-century extensions, its original plan suggests a much earlier foundation of a house with direct entry and opposed doors. Alterations, however, have left a hearth-passage plan typical of later centuries. Melbourne House, in South Street, also dates from the mid-eighteenth century; as does Holly Bank, on Scalby Road, formerly a farmhouse whose site is said to date back to the fourteenth century.

Later-dated properties of distinction in Scalby include Yew Court Terrace across the road from the Nag's Head public house. A striking row of symmetrical commercial and residential properties built for Mr W. Tingle Brown, with end gables on the outer two, and a central tower with open cupola supporting a domed cap on turned wooden pillars, enclosing the middle residences.

At one time the terrace included the blacksmith shop of Mr John G. Boddy, councillor and staunch Wesleyan, which was later taken over by his eldest son, also named John,

Yew Court Terrace fronting the High Street. Built by Mr Tingle Brown of Yew Court, it was a mix of commercial and residential property. The shop which first opened in 1849, was then in the ownership of Wallis & Blakeley, who celebrated the event by giving away to the children 'sticks of barley sugar'. It closed in 1926, taken over by Rowntree

who was a well-respected singer hereabouts. There was also the house and commercial premises of Mr Cross the tailor, who used his front parlour as a fitting room, and who had two apprentices, the brothers Alf and Harry Hodgson. Finally the terrace was completed with the corner shop, originally opened by Wallis & Blakeley and later taken over by Rowntrees of Scarborough.

There was of course, and still is, the schoolhouse at Church Becks, abutting the lower boundary of the churchyard. The first village school was built in Scalby in 1828, when the Revd C.A. Thurlow was a vicar. This was a modest one-room building next to the west wall of the churchyard, and seems to have served fairly well as a day school and Sunday school for some forty years, when a larger building was erected in stone on the same site in 1861. This consisted of a lofty, well-lit schoolroom measuring 52 ft by 18 ft which could be divided when necessary by curtains suspended from iron rods, and an adjoining schoolhouse.

A clock over the school door was the only public clock in the district. Near this was the school bell, hung high above the playground between tall wooden poles. These offered a perpetual challenge to small boys to swarm up and ring the bell. The penalty for success was six of the best!

As the number of pupils increased it was deemed necessary to add a classroom to the main building. This was erected by Mr John Robinson, the village mason, at a cost of £80. The school catered not only for the village children but for the whole surrounding districts, pupils coming from as far as Keld Runnels (Scalby Nabs), Throxenby, Scalby Mills, Suffield and Burniston. There was no public transport in those days and the journeys to and from school had to be made on foot. Nor were there any school meals – the children from a distance brought their lunch with them.

The schoolhouse, Scalby, rebuilt in 1861. It was
here that Mr J.D. Tickle taught for forty years

It is recorded that on one occasion none of the Burniston children put in an appearance
at school. Later, on being questioned about this truancy, it was found that this was due to
the fact that a ship laden with coal had gone aground at Burniston, and in the manner of
nineteenth-century 'wreckers', the children and parents had 'looted' the cargo for their
own use in the coming winter months!

In 1861, when the new building was ready for occupancy, the then schoolmaster, Mr
Henry Mayhew, whose name can still be seen scratched on one of the windows, was
transferred from the old school. His task could not have been easy, for he had to teach
eighty-six children of all ages, including fourteen under six years old. He died in 1876 and
was followed by a Mr Johnson, during whose brief occupation of the post – about five
years – the number rose to over one hundred, but by now he was assisted by a pupil
teacher.

Mr Johnson was followed by Mr William Yates, who held the position of headmaster
for only two years. Then in 1883 came Mr John Tickle, who intended this to be a
temporary appointment but remained in it for almost forty years. During that time, in
addition to being headmaster, he was church organist and choirmaster, Sunday school
superintendent, secretary to the Reading Room, clerk to the parish council (and afterwards
to the Urban District Council) and secretary of the Scalby and Newby Show. This last post
he held for forty-two years, and saw the show expand from a 'foal show' in the school
playground to a major event in the district calendar.

After ninety years of use the National School, as it had become, eventually became too small for the ever increasing population, and was replaced by two fine buildings in Newby. The old church school continued in use for the under-eleven's until 1950, when Newby Primary School was opened and all the educational needs of the children were transferred to that village.

Scalby also possessed, and still does to some extent, a number of small cottages and lesser farmhouses of good stone. The former, originally erected in terraces or singly, were built of local materials and thatched, and had their exterior walls whitewashed annually. Unfortunately many disappeared in the early years of this century.

Most building stone came from nearby Cloughton, which improves with weathering. Scalby has no good stone of its own – the quarry for the village was at Cumboots, but the stone is very soft and crumbly. A second smaller quarry existed above Prospect House, and provided lesser material for road repair and meaner dwellings.

Later, bricks came into use and were at one time handmade. Such bricks can be found in the Duchy property, Lancaster House, in the High Street. The bricks were made from clay obtained, it is said, from a patch of land in what is now the Park, off Station Road. Most nineteenth-century brick, however, was brought in, no doubt on the newly introduced railway, and from this period the character and appearance of Scalby housing changed.

Finally, one property that is now demolished but is still commemorated on a building erected on the site, deserves a mention – Keld's Hospital Almshouses. Originally erected in 1647, today two plaques on a cottage along the High Street, opposite the 'gates' of Yew Court, mark the position of what was 'a Hospital for the residence and maintenance of four poor widows or widowers of Scalby, Newby, or Throxenby'.[28] Cole further states, 'The building devoted to this purpose is a thatched one, with stone mullioned windows, containing four apartments'.[29] Short on detail, the property actually consisted of four self-contained rooms, two on the ground floor and two above, which were reached by outside stairways.

By 1829 they had 'degenerated' to a point where, in 1854, they had to be rebuilt as a 'plain two-storey house'.[30] As living conditions improved, poor widows and widowers could not be found to occupy the dwellings, and the redundant almshouses were finally pulled down in 1909 as one of the plaques records.

It was Christopher Keld who built and endowed the almshouses. He resided at Newby Hall, erected 'in the true hall-like style of the period, possessing stone mullion windows, and in front a porch, over which were the ornamental balls, or heads, so commonly used in buildings of that time'.[31] Today all that remains of this mansion is the name, the balls (thought lost but unearthed and placed on the stone gateposts of the farm that replaced Newby Hall), and a stone carved with the Keld's family arms and the date 1660 taken from the original house and retained in the fabric of the farmstead.

An endowment, couched in the following terms, bequeathed on the death of Christopher Keld, provided for the inmates of his 'Hospital', and consisted of six acres of land in Scalby (valued at £16 5s. 0d. in 1905:[32])

Item. 'I give to four of the poorest Widows, or Widowers, that now are, or successively shall be, one after another, within the Towns of Scalby, Newby, and Throstanby, One House, newly builded, and joyned, to the West end of the house, of

John Marshal, in Scalby, with a Garden-place, at the West end of the same house, containing in length, twenty feet; and in breadth, fourteen feet; And two Closes, the One, in the Occupation of Adam Farside, abutting upon his Dwelling House, towards the North; the Ground of William Hird, towards the South; the King's street towards the East, and upon Scalby Hay, towards the West; The other, in the occupation of Robert Balk, abutting upon the ground of William Hird, towards the north, and the Ground of Thomas Redhead, towards the South; To be, and remain, to the same use for ever. The said four poor Widows or Widowers, as they shall succeed one after another, to be chosen by my Sons, Thomas Keld, Edward Keld, and Christopher Keld, their heirs, and Children's Children; and after them, the said poor people to be chosen, nominated, and appointed, by the Vicars of Scalby successively, one after another for ever.'

In conclusion, it may be interesting to include here an account of one of Scalby's 'architectural' landmarks which, while itself is not a building, nevertheless when first erected elicited some degree of comment to the amusement of readers of the *Scarborough Post*.

SCALBY JUBILEE MEMORIAL FOUNTAIN

To the Editor of the Scarborough Post.

Sir, – Two gentlemen on bicycles might have been seen a few days ago travelling down one of the principal streets of Scalby. When opposite to the present writer – who was taking his morning constitutional – they jumped off and one of them said – 'I give it up'. As this remark seemed addressed to me, I said 'What do you give up?' 'The Scalby puzzle,' was the reply 'to find the Jubilee Memorial Fountain.' I am going that way, said I, and shall be glad to show it to you, so the two – whose names it appeared were Mr Envy and Mr Liar – followed, wheeling their machines. 'There it is,' said I, pointing with pardonable pride to the splendid fountain. 'That!' said Mr Liar, 'we saw that thing before but thought it was the first grave stone erected in the little burying ground which we supposed to belong to the chapel across the road. We sir,' continued Mr L., 'are connected with the Press, and have come to Scalby expressly to see this memorial fountain.'

They both appeared (judging by the colour of their noses) to have had a close connection with a whisky press for some considerable time. 'I suppose this site has been selected,' said Mr Envy, 'because it enables your constable to keep an eye upon the fountain. No doubt he can sleep with one eye open?' 'Perhaps he can,' said I, 'but why should he exercise that gift if he has it?' 'Well,' said Mr Envy, 'some evil-disposed person who owns a donkey and cart might, under cloud of night, lay hands on the fountain, and bear it away to parts unknown.'

'This is no doubt another gift from Mr Ellis to the village,' said Mr Liar. 'No,' said I, 'read the inscription, it is erected by the parishioners. Alone we did it! *gaudeamus igitur!*' (I thought this Latin tag might subdue the two pressmen, but they showed little perceptible shrinkage.) 'We are in hopes that this stupendous undertaking might be brought to a prosperous conclusion before the end of this century, and the water duly laid on,' I continued.

The Jubilee Memorial Fountain, Scalby: 'Erected by the Parishioners of Scalby to Commemorate the Diamond Jubilee of Her Most Gracious Majesty, Queen Victoria R.I. 20th June 1857'

'I hear,' said Mr Liar, 'it is to be opened – when finished – by one of the great ones of the earth, and that it is to yield the best of tea for three hours for the benefit of the women and children of the parish, everyone to bring his or her mug. Then for two hours the fountain shall run Kops Ale with a sketch of sperrits in it for the benefit of the teetotalers. And then, up to midnight, whisky negus for the topers.' 'Speaking of these good things,' said Mr Envy, 'where can we get some refreshment in this historical town of yours?' 'At the "Nag his Head," just mention my name – Mr Cobbe Dobbs – to uncle Jarvis and he will be sure to attend to your wants. He has a great respect for gentlemen of the Press.'

'Well,' said Mr Envy, as he walked round for the last time, 'I never saw a fountain like this before, and I hope I shall never see the like of it again *rideamus igitur*!' With that the two personified vices gave the spur to their 'prancing steeds' and departed, laughing loudly. I looked earnestly at a large pebble at my feet but forebore to throw it. Poor wretches! thought I, they are full of bitter envy and anger because they must soon return to their fountainless town again.

What will Macaulay's New Zealander think of our fountain when he takes a run through England after sketching the ruins of St Paul's. What manner of men were those Scalby parishioners at the end of the 19th century, he may ask himself. Intensely loyal they must have been, or they would never have thought of erecting such a splendid memorial to their Queen. Rich also, beyond the dreams of avarice, they surely were, or how could they have subscribed a sum sufficient to erect such a noble monument! Well, said the sweet poetess, Eliza Cook, of those grand fellows:–

There's a glorious charter, deny it who can
Breathed in the words I am a–

SCALBY MAN!

NOTES

1. YAS, *Cal. Pat.* 1461–7, p. 376.
2. Kelly's *Directory North Riding of Yorkshire*, 1905.
3. Bulmer's *History & Directory North Yorkshire*, 1890.
4. Ibid.
5. Kelly's, 1905.
6. Cole, John, *Historical Sketches of Scalby, Burniston & Cloughton*, 1829.
7. *Scarborough Mercury*, Nov. 1957.
8. Robertson, A., *Atkinson Grimshaw*, Phaidon, 1988.
9. Cole, op. cit.
10. Chapman, M & B., *The Pierrots of The Yorkshire Coast*, Hutton Press, 1988.
11. Ibid., p. 43.
12. Ibid.
13. Ibid., p. 45.
14. Ibid.
15. Ibid.
16. Ibid., p. 48.
17. Ibid., p. 49.
18. Ibid.
19. Ibid.
20. Ibid., pp. 49– 50.
21. Ibid., p. 50.
22. Ibid.
23. Ibid., p. 51.
24. Ibid.
25. Feinstein, C.H., *York 1831–1981: 150 Years of Scientific Endeavour & Social Change*, p. 40, 1981.
26. Cole, op. cit.
27. *Scarborough Mercury*, Oct. 1957.
28. Cole, John, op. cit.
29. *Scarborough Mercury*, Nov 1957.
30. Whellan & Co., *North Riding Yorkshire Directory*, 1859.
31. Cole, op. cit.
32. Kelly's, 1905.

CHAPTER THREE

Church and Chapel

The parish church of St Laurence stands, as described by Cole, 'upon a gentle elevation, at the western extremity of the village, near the Hackness road, and from several points of view is a very picturesque object'.[1] In parts, it is the oldest building in Scalby.

There was a church here of some description as early as the twelfth century. During the anarchy of King Stephen's reign, it came into the possession of Eustace, son of John, who held the castle of Malton against the king.[2] Eustace Fitzjohn, with the consent of Archbishop Thurstan, granted the church to Bridlington Priory in 1135, the grant being confirmed by King Stephen and later, Henry II.[3]

Historically, the priory has always held the church appropriated,[4] and there is a record of a vicar being instituted early in 1236.[5] In the year 1547 Edward VI granted the rectory an advowson – the right to present a vicar – worth then £6 13s. 6d.,[6] to the Dean and Chapter of Norwich Cathedral,[7] who have ever since been patrons.[8]

The west tower of Scalby Church erected in the fifteenth century and rebuilt in 1683

Scalby Church from the south

The parish bounds, at one time, stretched from just beyond Ravenscar in the north down to the boundary of St Mary's, Scarborough, in the south. This continued until 1874, when Cloughton, Burniston and Staintondale were formed into the district chapelry of Cloughton.[9] Since then Staintondale-with-Ravenscar has become a parish in its own right, and is now a United Benefice with Scalby church. In 1235 there was a chapel in Burniston which came under the control of Scalby, and by 1298 a further chapel existed at Cloughton, also under the control of Scalby.[10]

Architecturally, St Laurence's Church consists of a chancel 35 ft 8 in by 17 ft 0 in; nave 35 ft 6 in by 20 ft 3 in; south aisle, porch and west tower. The total length is 89 ft 0 in; all measurements being internal.[11]

The earliest work remaining in the building dates from about 1180, when the south nave arcade and the chancel arch were built. The chancel was reconstructed in the early years of the following century, and in the fifteenth century the nave arches were apparently rebuilt together with much of the north wall. Late in the sixteenth or early seventeenth century, the present west tower was erected and some work appears to have been undertaken in the chancel towards the close of the latter century. The church was drastically restored in 1887 by 'private subscription and the produce of a bazaar',[12] and the south aisle and porch are entirely modern. The east wall of the chancel has also been rebuilt and the south wall refaced.

The chancel has a modern three-lighted east window, although it was said in 1848 that the jambs were originally 'Early English' and that there was a date, 1685, carved in the head suggesting that there had been a continuity throughout the years.[13] In the north wall there are two thirteenth-century lancet windows and a further one blocked. A sealed door on this side led to a destroyed vestry, of which traces are still visible on the outside wall. In the south wall are two other lancet windows. The chancel arch dates from 1180 and springs from responds having each three attached shafts, the centre one of bowtel form and all bearing moulded capitals with square abaci.

The east window glass dates from 1960, and was designed, painted and made by Francis Stephens, the London-based glazier, and erected by Messrs Lazenby's. It depicts the story of St Laurence and commemorates the incumbency of the Revd E.A. Flowerday, vicar of Scalby between 1950 and 1959.

This window replaced a window dedicated to Timothy Hardcastle, of Scalby Hall, and given by his widow, Mrs Betsy Hardcastle, in 1854, which depicted respectively the Baptism, Last Supper and Crucifixion of Christ.[14] The floor below the window and beneath the altar is ancient, and the tiles, lozenged-shaped, are coloured yellow and azure (blue). In the north-east corner there is a thirteenth-century stone grave-slab with a floriated cross carved upon it in low relief.

At one time the pews in the chancel were placed transversely north to south, effectively shutting out the view of the Lord's Table from worshippers in the nave. They were consequently moved to their present position possibly in the eighteenth century; a note in the parish register states that in 1767 the pews in the church were rebuilt and the body of

South arcade: wooden poor box of Jacobean date below the inscription of medieval origin which reads 'Pra Remember The Poor'

Front and side elevation of the alms box, Scalby church

the church underdrawn. Finally, there are two sedilia of equal height under a square head – 'but utterly unworthy of note'.[15]

The nave is of three bays, and in the north wall are three two-light windows with quatrefoil tracery, all modern. The external buttresses of this wall date from the fifteenth century, and in the middle one can be found the heads of two nails, hand-forged, one above the other, placed there, it is said, by the family of a local blacksmith who died too poor to afford a headstone. The nails mark the close proximity of his grave.

The south arcade has cylindrical piers with moulded bases and capitals with square abaci of the same period as the chancel arch – Norman – although one authority suggests they may be of a slightly later date, and belong to the 'Transitional' period.[16] Interestingly, the eastern-most capital has a crude decoration of foliage carved on it, suggestive of a late twelfth- or early thirteenth-century date. From the capitals, a kind of pyramidal ornament springs three or four inches up the side of each arch. The arches themselves appear to have been reconstructed in the fifteenth century, and are not quite sprung centrally from the middle pier. Two further points of interest are the carved wooden figure of St Laurence attached to the respond, or half pillar at the west end of the nave behind the verger's pew, and a carved inscription on the first pillar of the nave facing the door which reads in local dialect, 'Pra Remember the Power' (Pray Remember the Poor). Below this, is situated a Jacobean poor box mounted on a heavy carved pillar of oak.

The communion table in the chancel, and the pulpit elsewhere are of the same period. The latter originally had a small door and was resited in its present position from a point further out in the body of the church. It is thought that the pulpit was manufactured by the same craftsman who made the pulpit in Hackness church. The Victoria County History suggests that the Scalby example is 'a poor specimen of Jacobean work'.[17] The south aisle has been entirely rebuilt and widened in modern times and has a three-light east window of little consequence.[18]

A plain circular font dates from the thirteenth century. In 1848 it was written, 'the font is probably Early English, but has little decided character; it presents however, a favourable instance of care, for instead of being whitewashed or painted, as is too usual, it is every year cleaned with a [scouring] stone. There is a Wedgwood-ware basin in the inside'.[19]

Externally, the square west tower is broken into three stages. The heavy buttresses at the angles having numerous offsets, and a subsidiary buttress is carried up the centre of the west face above which are inserted two grotesque gargoyles with fully distended mouths – well adapted for 'spitting' off water. The lower storeys are without windows; the belfry windows are of two lights, once transomed, without cusps, but with incised work filling the space between the heads of the lights and the hood moulding.[20] The parapet is embattled. The stairs run in a projection on the north-east face which rises higher than the parapet, and is surmounted by a weather-vane of heavy copper which represents the grid-iron on which St Laurence was martyred. Although of predominately fifteenth-century appearance, the tower was rebuilt in 1683 as witnessed by a date carved on one of the windows which also includes two partial names, 'Thomas ——, Samewell ——, Churchwardens'.

The obliteration of surnames on church inscriptions is not an uncommon feature at this period in history, and reflects the changes in 'Church' politics occurring at that time.

The earliest legible gravestone in Scalby
churchyard, commemorating the vicar, John
Bosse, who died in 1696

The belfry contains a peal of bells, three of which are ancient, dated and inscribed;
however, one was recast and is further lettered:

> Gloria in Exelsis Deo, et in Terra pax, anno Pacis 1919.
> W. Hesmondhalgh, W.H.L. Holdsworth, E. Ward, Ch'Wardens.

The other inscriptions read, '1674 Concorde nos estote vos Ebor'; '1674 Breve et
irrepabile tempus SS Ebor'; '1674 Omnia mors poscit, Johannes Bosse, Vicarius'.[21]

The grave of John Bosse, vicar of Scalby from 1663 to 1690, still exists, tucked away
beneath the tower's south wall. It is the oldest legible gravestone and is inscribed in Latin
with the following verse:

> Here lies the body of John Bosse
> lately vicar of this church who died
> on the 20th day of April 1696
> If God be for us,
> Who shall be against us.

His stone faces west instead of the usual east, a common orientation for clerics, to
ensure that on the 'Resurrection Morning', as parson, they will rise facing their flock.

The grave of schoolmaster Mr J.D. Tickle (1887–1959) and his wife Muriel. Mr Tickle was also organist and choirmaster at Scalby for some years, receiving in payment at one time the sum of £5.00 per annum

In 1961 three more bells were added to the belfry, bringing the number to six, and a team of ringers was soon begun, originally trained by Bert Sutton. In addition to the church bells, there is an enthusiastic group of handbell ringers, which started in 1967 when Mr Alan Grundy was given an octave of bells. The ringers have gone on from strength to strength and now have thirty-six handbells and often travel throughout the area demonstrating their 'art'.[22]

Returning to the tower's architecture, the coping of the battlements, now confined to the north side, and excluding the tower parapet, have a return; 'a little circumstance which is worth noticing here, because it is the only church, except Filey . . . where it occurs'.[23] Although steeply pitched, the chancel roof was once flatter.[24]

In 1848 the authors Revd G.A. Poole, vicar of Welford and John Hugall, architect and secretary of the Yorkshire Archaeological Society, noted in conclusion to their description of Scalby church,

> although there are few eminently good features, yet if we could add to this history the restoration of the chancel windows, the throwing down of the galleries,[25] and the substitution of open seats for closed pues [pews], we should be disposed to class this among the more favourable specimens of unassuming village churches.[26]

The churchyard, which must be one of the most pleasant and best kept in the country, was extended in the 1950s. The older part offers considerable interest to the local historian. Unfortunately the weather has defaced the oldest tombstones so that the inscriptions are undecipherable; notwithstanding that, burials have occurred at Scalby over a much longer period than the oldest of graves.

As far back as 1448 one William Gower, of Cloughton, willed to be buried in the church. And in 1647 'Christopher Keld, of Scarburgh, Gent' – undoubtedly an ancestor of the Christopher Keld who built and endowed the almshouses of Scalby, possibly even his father – was buried at the east end of the chancel.

Apart from these and older graves, other tombs of interest in and around the churchyard are those of Enos Bravender Thompson, situated over to the west of the tower, and that of James Law, who was shot dead by a revengeful smuggler as he rode through Burniston in 1823. The attendance at his funeral is said to have been the greatest ever known at Scalby. An entry in the parish register under that year, headed 'James Law. Staintondale. February 24th – aged 60', throws some further light on the event:

This worthy & Much respected man, was shot by William Mead of Burniston . . . The same date, as he passed his [Mead's] House, early on Friday Morning, the 14th February . . . James Law had obtained a Verdict in the Court of Exchequer, upon a Charge of Smuggling about the month of June 1822, and he brought an Action against Mead for Wilfull & Corrupt Perjury in the Cause, of which perjury he was found Guilty in the Court of King's Bench on Thursday the 19th Day of December, 1822 after a Trial of 12 Hours – In a short Time after Mead was bailed by Government [he] then returned to Burniston, & shot his antagonist. Mead was committed to York Castle on Friday, the 28th Day of February. 1823 –

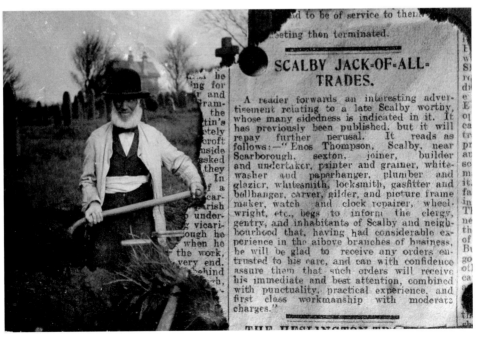

The much beloved Scalby character, Enos Thompson, engaged in his work of grave-digging

Re a/c 8142

To the
Yorkshire Penny Bank
Scarborough

Pay Enos Thompson on production of this card the sum of 17/4 on the first of every month commencing Jan 1st 1908

W. Cautley Robinson ..... *Vicar*
Wm Hanquite .....} *Churchwardens*
W. J. Brown ..... }

The payment card of Mr Enos Thompson

It is interesting to note that Mrs Abram, Milly Kidd's great-grandmother, and her husband John Abram, who carried on a dairy business at Cockrah Farm, Burniston, at that time, were called as witnesses at the trial which followed the dramatic shooting tragedy of James Law at Burniston in 1823. The incident itself was recalled in the *Scarborough Mercury* on the occasion of the one hundredth anniversary (February 1923).

Concerning Enos Thompson, he was a man of many parts – a Scalby craftsman of Victorian times much revered in the village for his skills, which, if we are to believe a contemporary advertisement, were practically limitless and included: paper hanging, painter and grainer, whitewasher, carver, gilder and picture-frame maker, plumber and glazier, whitesmith, locksmith, gas fitter and bell-hanger, builder and joiner, watch and clock repairer, wheelwright, as well as sexton and grave-digger, for which he was paid, on production of a card at the Yorkshire Penny Bank each month, 17s. 4d. His family still live in the area and his grandson, at the present time[27] holds the office of churchwarden. On Enos Thompson's death in 1912 a newspaper report of his burial provided further facts about his life:

Mr Thompson was connected with Scalby church for a number of years as sexton, clerk and bell-ringer, and even after his place as sexton and clerk was taken by the late Mr Charles Ralph, who died about two months ago, he still continued to toll a bell.

A strange fact in connection with his death was that while a bell-ringing practice was in full swing on Tuesday night at about 9.15, the rope of the bell which Mr Thompson used to ring broke, and it was afterwards learned that this happened almost simultaneously with his death.

In his capacity of sexton he made nearly every grave there is at present in the new cemetery. He had a splendid memory, and while able to entertain people from a large store of reminiscences, he could answer accurately the dates on which almost any event of local importance took place within the last thirty years.

His abilities extended in nearly every direction and he could repair a watch equally as well as the church organ. It has been stated that he had a notice published setting forth the various kinds of work he could do, but it is said that his modesty would not permit him to do anything like this. The real fact is that over twenty-five years ago when Sir Frank Lockwood (then Mister) was in Scalby he was greatly amused to hear of the number of trades Mr Thompson was proficient in, and after asking Mr Thompson's permission he compiled a list and sent it to *Truth*. The list afterwards appeared in many of the morning papers, and eventually it gained publicity in an American journal.

Finally, of note in the churchyard of St Laurence's Church is the sundial, on a pedestal opposite the porch, bearing the inscription that it was the gift of George Dickinson in the 'Year of Our Lord, 1690'.

Of other religious institutions in Scalby little is recorded. A small stone-built chapel of eighteenth-century date standing in the High Street, presumably became too restrictive for the needs of the congregation, and in the following century (*c.* 1880[28]) it became the 'Reading Room' of the village. Today it is a cottage of distinction only recognizable by its unique architecture and ornamentation similar to the surviving belvedere of the original Low Hall; the inscription over the door, which no doubt told of its former use, is sadly defaced.

The newer Wesleyan chapel in North Street was erected in 1873, and is a fine example of the mid-Victorian mason's craft. The Primitive Methodist formerly met in their own building on Low Street, built in 1894 and opened the following year. This plain, brick chapel, somewhat asymmetrical with a small bell-cote, was demolished in 1967, and

The Methodist church in Low Street around 1906. It was demolished in 1967 and a bungalow now stands on the site

latterly they met for worship in the Temperance Hall near to the Wesleyan chapel, which before its redundancy housed a second 'Reading' or 'Newspaper Room' and a billiard hall.

The Temperance Movement in Scalby had a fascinating history, and its establishment in the village was due in no uncertain terms to the efforts of a number of the leading lights of the district who championed its ideals. A newspaper article commissioned and published on the occasion of the opening of the Temperance Hall in 1894 most admirably traced its growth:

Over forty years ago, when the Temperance Movement in England was comparatively in its infancy, several meetings were held in a cottage near the church at Scalby, the outcome of which was the formation of the Scalby Temperance Society. The little band of workers, including Mr H.M. Cross, JP; Mr John Hodgson; and the late Mr William Thompson, whose efforts were first devoted to the cause, were determined to succeed, and overcoming the numerous obstacles presenting themselves, they progressed in such a satisfactory manner that today the Society has a membership of over sixty adults, and a Band of Hope of which eighty children are members. This latter was commenced by Mrs Woodhouse, of Scarborough, about ten years ago when staying in the village, and its meetings, which are held fortnightly, are of the most successful character. In a village the size of Scalby this is an exceedingly pleasing state of affairs, and, as Mr John Boddy, the president, whose whole heart is in the work, assures us, 'there is no telling what amount of good work has been done by our Society, as young men who have been members have gone to various parts of England, and we often hear good and cheering news from them'.

The cottage in which the temperance cause in Scalby was cradled soon became too small, and a look-out was kept by the managing committee for more commodious premises. This resulted in the purchase of the property that has been used for the meetings of the Society until the beginning of this year. It was a building situated almost opposite the Nag's Head public-house, and facing the road leading from the station, and thus being in a central position, when it came into the market about forty years ago, it was determined to purchase it. Mr John Hodgson was then one of the leading men in the village, and took a very active part in the work. The property was bought for about sixty pounds, the purchaser being Mr H.M. Cross, Mr John Hodgson, Mr Robert Coates, and Mr David Robinson. Much alteration, however, was required to be made before the building was suitable for the purposes it was intended for. The lower part had up to that time been used as a blacksmith's shop, and was occupied by a man named Armstrong, the room over the shop being used for living purposes by the Armstrong family, access being gained by a flight of stone steps at the outside. Immediately adjoining was the village pinfold, whilst in front, until they suddenly disappeared about thirty year ago, were the disused stocks, which in this later period served only as a reminder of former days, and became a resting place for the weary.

When the temperance party bought this building, they knocked the floor out, and made the whole into one room, and erected a small gallery at one end, which was ascended by means of a staircase inside the building, the old stone steps outside having been removed. At the other end of the room a platform was erected, and then a plentiful supply of forms [seats] being obtained, the society commenced to hold its meetings in this place, and continued to do so until January of this year, when the old building was pulled down to make way for the more commodious and modern building which was opened on Monday.

Some years ago, when the society had managed to pay off about thirty pounds of the cost of their hall, it was decided that the remaining thirty pounds should be taken up in one pound shares by the members. This was done, but about five or six years ago a bazaar was held to clear off this portion, so that the hall might become altogether the property of the society. So earnestly did the members work that the result was a brilliant success, as altogether forty pound was realised, thus leaving the society, after paying off the debt, with ten pounds in hand.

With the rapid growth of the membership, it was again very evident that the old hall was far too small for their requirements. On several occasions it had been crowded to excess, and at the last meeting held before the pulling down of the old hall was commenced, seven adults signed the pledge.

In Mr J.E. Ellis, MP, of Wrea Head, Scalby, the society has for years had one of the staunchest and most liberal supporters, and the new Temperance Hall has been built entirely at this gentleman's cost, and it is not only an architectural adornment to this part of the village, but will enable the society to widely extend its ranks and prosecute in a more vigorous manner the cause for which it was founded.

The new building was commenced on February 1st, the builders being Messrs Padbury & Son, Trinity Works, Scarborough, and the architects Messrs Malcolm, Stark & Rowntree, of Glasgow. It comprises on the ground floor a large class-room, smoke-room, reading-room, and a small library, and on the upper floor a hall capable of holding 150 persons. This is approached by a wide staircase, whilst a small kitchen is attached to the hall for use in case of teas, etc. The new hall is built of red bricks, with stone facings and tile roofing, the interior being fitted up in quite a modern style, and with such a suitable building the work of the Scalby Society, which is quite unsectarian in its character, should make rapid progress.

Finally, a chapter on 'Church and Chapel' would surely be incomplete without an account of the parish registers and the clergy who compiled them. The registers were started in 1556, and record the first burial for that year as Isabel Wasneth on 1 September. This may possibly have been penned by Henry Kay, clerk, who was inducted as parish priest on 24 October 1554.

The first record of a priest at Scalby is that of Master Henry Devon, in 1238. He was presented by the Prior and Convent of Bridlington and took up his post on 19 January. However, it is thought that either a William or Walter held the living previous to this.

Following the death of Henry Devon, Master Roger de Schartheburgh took the vacancy of Scalby, instituted on 17 July 1244. He was also abbot of Whitby, appointed on the death of John of Evesham, in 1222. Born at Scarborough, the historian Charlton wrote of Roger:

he resided many years in the cell at Middleburgh church, whence arose the universal veneration every one in that part of the country had for him, and the many donations made to the monastery of Whitby. He was undoubtably a man of great abilities, and no abbot of Whitby ever equalled him, or so much advanced the interest of the monastery . . . Roger spoke more, but was an upright honest man, without dissimulation, who regularly performed all the duties of religion; free, open, and devoid of pride, his behaviour engaged and endeared him to all with whom he had any dealings; and the charities he bestowed were always so well chosen and timed, that they added to his reputation, and gained him fresh supplies of money and continual liberalities from the whole country for miles round; and though it does not appear that he was ever called up to Parliament as a Lord; yet no nobleman in England was more revered and respected. During the twenty-two years of his reign, he raised the monastery of Whitby to the full zenith of its glory; as it never appeared so illustrious as when governed by Roger, nor even after his death did it ever gain any considerable additions either in riches or power.[29]

William de Besynby succeeded Roger de Schartheburgh on 2 July 1319. He died thirty years later, in 1349, and was buried in Scalby churchyard. The priest next appointed in that year was Robert de Sutton, who resigned for the living of Stillingfleet church soon after, as the name Richard de Wrelleton, or Wrelton, is recorded as chaplain of Scalby on 28 May 1349.

In succession there then followed: John Saylevur de Ulram (13 October 1365); John, son of Adam de Burniston (15 December 1374), who resigned for the living of Lethley church; John de Cave (11 January 1380) who resigned for a position in the chantry of Wykeham, founded by John de Wicham on the 'site of the Church of *All Saints*, which was taken down, being ruinous and decayed, and dedicated to the Virgin Mary & St Helen';[30] Robert Dalby, priest, instituted 26 March 1392; William de Hollym (26 April 1408), who resigned in favour of the chantry of Brampstone; Richard Lesset (18 December 1409); Richard Nafferton, who resigned; Henry Smyth, priest, inducted 28 July 1439; a second Henry Smyth (possibly the son) followed him on 4 December 1458, who died in the year 1480, and was buried in the 'quire' of Scalby church. Then came William Greenhow (10 April 1480) who resigned; William Ibson, instituted 13 May 1501; Robert Storke, who died in office; Henry Kaye, clerk, instituted 2 October 1554, and resigned; Master Richard Jenkinson (22 July 1556), resigned; Robert Wood, clerk, instituted 3 November 1576, and on his resignation, William de Buckton was installed 16 May 1586; John Trowsdale, clerk, and farmer, of the rectory, was instituted 14 June 1587 and on his death, William Taylor succeeded on 8 February 1588.

When William Taylor died, Thomas Bell was instituted 6 July 1593. His will records, 'Thomas Bell, of Scawby, clerk, – His body to the earth. 1621'. Cole writes, 'Mr Bell appears to have bestowed much pains on the register.' In 1653 an Act of Parliament decreeded that the register should be taken out of the hands of the minister and placed in the care of an 'elected' Parish Registrar, and so we find noted under 26 October 1653, 'Edward Matthew of Scalby being chosen by the inhabitants of the same to be their parish Register uppon the taking of this oath will and faithfully . . . perform the said office . . .'.

On the death of Thomas Bell, George Harrison was inducted vicar of Scalby on 13 December 1621. Later George Jay, or Gay, took the vacant living on 23 June 1631. Following his death, Nicholas Howlett was instituted 14 August 1634. On his cession, William Mompesson came to Scalby in September 1663.

The name of Revd William Mompesson is perhaps more readily associated with the great plague of 1665, which, apart from causing great havoc in London, practically decimated the village of Eyam, in Derbyshire, where Mompesson was then vicar. It was his prompt action in isolating the village that saved the surrounding district from being infected by the contagion. Many have speculated whether the method he employed to achieve this was one he learnt in his twelve months as priest of Scalby, as forty years previous, in 1625, the plague that then swept through England, started in the neighbourhood.

Cole wrote:

It was attributed to a sea-faring man, just returned from the East Indies; whose wife being landed at Cloughton, appeared on the following Sunday in the church of Scalby, habited in black silk. Whether the contagion was conveyed in this dress, then put on for the purpose of attending divine worship, or the disease, from which she had apparently recovered, yet lurked in her frame cannot be positively ascertained, but certain it is that it quickly spread its baneful effects around, as many of the congregation were suddenly infected, became sick, and fell in their pews, which caused the officiating clergyman to desist from *preaching*, and put into *practice*, his labour of love. The pestilential contagion was soon disseminated over this and the neighbouring villages, and but few escaped its ravages:[31] the family of a medical man then resident at Scalby it is reported, preserved themselves, through the blessing of Providence, from its sickening consequences by alternately fasting, and eating every morning rue and figs.

It is curious to observe that a lady of Scalby, who was, at this calamitious period, near the time of her accouchement, and fearing she would take the disorder, caused a cow-house, situated in a pasture, near the village, to be fitted up as the chamber of her delivery, and on the emergency of the moment, it was hung round with the undressed, but no less serviceable, skins of sheep; and in this very humble abode, she was, through the care of Providence, sheltered from the effects of the Plague, and recovered her wonted health.[32]

During the time of this plague, Sir Thomas Posthumous Hoby, of Hackness Hall, arranged for 'wain-loads' of wheat and foodstuffs to be left at the Rosette Inn, in Newby. The inhabitants of Scalby and Newby were then invited to come and help themselves. Unfortunately, before they could avail themselves of this generosity, it is said, 'strangers' removed the food, so that by the time Scalby and Newby folk arrived nothing remained. This event gave rise to a doggerel hereabouts which became known as 'The Scalby Grace' (recounted below), and it was this action in requesting food to be left outside the village for the use of the inhabitants, which the Revd Mompesson copied forty years later at Eyam.

> O Lord our God send down Thy word,
> With trusty sword and sickles,
> To cut the throats of all these folks,
> That's robbed us of our vittals.

On the cessation of Revd Mompesson, John Bosse was inducted in 1663; he resigned, and on his death, was buried in the churchyard as we have noted. In the year 1690 Samuel Wilson was instituted vicar of Scalby; following his death, William Hollis held the living from 1708. It was this Revd W. Hollis who inscribed in the registers at the time of the baptism of Mabel Trott, on 23 May 1714, 'a ridiculous name given her, became she was born on Mayday'. He died in office, and on 8 October 1737, William Ward, AB, was inducted.

It was during his incumbency that Archbishop Herring of York, newly appointed in 1742, called for a survey of the diocese in the following terms:

Good Brother,

Being by God's Providence call'd to a new Diocese, with the Circumstances whereof I am very much unacquainted, I shall hold myself extreamly oblig'd to You for your Assistance in the Administration of it. To render that more effectual, I send to you and the rest of my Clergy the following Paper of Questions; a clear and satisfactory return to which under the Hand of every several Minister and delivered to my Secretary, or the Register, at the Time of my Visitation, will make me much better acquainted with the Circumstances of this large Diocese, then I cou'd be by any other way, save that of a Parochial Visitation, which is out of my power to take.

You will therefore be so good as to gratify my request herein, and as this is the only design of my sending these Enquiries to You, You may rest perfectly assured, that no other use shall be made of them, but for my own Information; and for that reason I will hope that You will deal very freely and plainly with me in your Answers to the several Questions.

To God's Favour and Blessing I heartily commend yourself, and your Labours in His Church, and remain,

> Reverend Sir,
> Your very affectionate Brother,
> Tho. Ebor

Kensington,
2nd May, 1743[33]

From the answers to the eleven questions the archbishop set out, we can obtain an interesting perspective on the religious and moral state of Scalby in the mid-eighteenth century.

For instance it was stated, 'There are about 207 families in ye Parish of which seven are Quakers, besides which there are no other Dissenters.' 'There is a Meeting House of Quakers in ye Parish [and] I believe licenced but of late their numbers are very much diminished, in so much that it is believed [that] they have no Assemblies [meetings], but on Sundays [and] not then constantly.' 'There is no School in the Parish.' 'There is no Alms House nor any Charitable Endowment only about three pounds a year is left to be distributed every Sunday in Bread to ye Poor, which is constantly done by ye Churchwarden [John Sedman & William Hodgson].'

Cole recalls that 'this valuable benefaction originated in the bequest of John Knowsley, which was carried into effect by his wife, Sarah Knowsley, who purchased land in Falsgrave, called Byard Wath, and appropriated it to this use'.[34] This distribution – or dole – of bread continued throughout the nineteenth century, and in 1905 it is recorded that,

'Bread to the value of £15 per year is distributed to the Poor every Sunday, and coals are given away at Christmas.'[35] Interestingly, the endowment of three pounds in money was a later legacy by one Adam Farside, who died in 1700. He gave the sum for the assistance of the poor to be distributed on 'three great Festivals of the Church'[36] – vicar Ward obviously confused the two and somewhat erroneously misled the archbishop in this statement.

At the time of Archbishop Herring's questionnaire, William Ward resided 'at Thornton [Dale] being Master of the Grammar School there'. At Scalby he said, 'I have a Residing curate [George Dodsworth] to whom I allow £25 a year, he does not reside in the Vicarage House'.

When asked, 'Do you know of any who come to Church in your Parish that are not Baptized? Or that being Baptized, and of a Competent Age, are not confirmed?' He stated, 'I know of none such.'

Later questions and answers dealt with the arrangement and times of church services. 'The Publick Service [is] read in the Parish twice every Lords Day, there being a chappel in the Parish where service is performed in the Morning once a Month and on other Sundays in the Afternoon.' 'The children are usually Catechised [instructed by question and answer in the religious faith] all Lent at which time they commonly appear.' 'The Sacrament [Communion] is administered four times a year at the Parish Church and four times a year at the Chappel the Communicants are pretty numerous, there might be about 200 at Easter last [1742].' 'Notice is constantly given of the Sacrament the Sunday before it is administered, but the Parishioners do not send in their Names; the sacrament has been refused to no Person. I have observed no defect in ye Discipline of the Church nor have I met with any particular difficulties in the discharge of my duty.'[37]

Following William Ward as vicar of Scalby, who died in office, came Thomas Preston, instituted 24 April 1773. He too died in office, and was succeeded in 1827 by the Revd Charles A. Thurlow, appointed by the Dean and Chapter of Norwich Cathedral, who had been patrons of the living on and off since 1554, taking over the right to appoint the vicar from the Prior and Convent of Bridlington Priory.

Clergy of the nineteenth century by and large enjoyed uneventful incumbencies at Scalby. This was a rural haven, tranquil, free from the controversies of Church and State which rocked some areas of the country in the mid years of this century. Suffice to say that their names are appended at the end of this chapter in the full list of incumbents, while the chapter itself is concluded with extracts about and recollections from the clergy, taken from one or two of the many newspaper accounts pasted into the Kidd album, which family itself was closely connected with the church in Scalby.

The Rev. William Cautley Robinson, BA, has just passed the thirty-fifth anniversary of his induction to the living of Scalby. He became Vicar of the Parish in January, 1876, and is today still faithfully serving the parishioners as minister to their spiritual needs.

'The population of the parish when I came [2 Feb 1876] was about eight hundred. It is now about 1,600. Since I have been at Scalby the Church has been twice renovated internally, and a valuable new organ, costing about £600 has been lately put in by the gift of the parishioners and other friends.

'The parish was purely agricultural as I first knew it. Now Scalby is a suburb of Scarborough. I recall when there was no railway, and since the line was opened the inhabitants have increased considerably. There have been three different occupants of The Hall in my time – Mr R. Green, followed by Mr W.R. Rudgard, then by Mr Bray, who died so recently. I have seen so many of the inhabitants of this parish pass away, so many indeed that it appears to be peopled almost entirely by a new generation.

'Enos Thompson has worshipped at the church throughout my time here, and there are also Mrs Kidd and Mrs Carr . . .

In the course of further conversation Mr Robinson said that he was married to Alice Roden [youngest daughter of the late Mr W. Roden, of Everleigh, Shropshire] in the year 1886, ten years after going to Scalby, and a service of silver plate was presented to him on his marriage by the parishioners.

At the presentation ceremony held in the village schoolroom Mr Enos Thompson 'presented the watch which was inscribed: "Presented to the Rev. W. Cautley Robinson, for 35 years vicar of Scalby, by his parishioners, as a token of esteem, 4th February, 1911"'.

Mr Ralph presented the chain, and Mrs Kidd the rose-bowl, which bore the inscription: 'Presented to the Rev. W. Cautley and Mrs Robinson, February 4th 1911, by the parishioners of Scalby, on the occasion of their silver wedding, 1886–1911'.

In making the presentation Mrs Kidd made a topical speech. She esteemed it an honour, she said, to be asked to make the presentation, and after Mr Thompson and Mr Ralph she came in a nice third (Laughter). She could not, however, present the bowl to Mrs Robinson and the vicar as well (Laughter). She would hand it to Mrs Robinson, and she wished them years and years of happiness. Mrs Robinson could put roses in out of their garden, and if Mr Robinson was not allowed to put them in, well she hoped he would get a good smell (Loud Laughter). Her husband, concluded Mrs Kidd, had the pleasure of fetching Mr and Mrs Robinson from their honeymoon 25 years ago – 'a carriage and pair, you know, and grey horses' (Loud Laughter).

SALE OF WORK. – On Wednesday, July 10th, a Sale of Work in aid of the renovation of the Church was held in the grounds of Scalby Hall, kindly lent by Mr and Mrs Rudgard, in a tent provided for the purpose. The stalls were presided over by Mrs Rudgard, assisted by Mrs P. Cook and Miss E. Rudgard; Mrs Magson was at the head of a stall which was chiefly the work of her young people's Sewing Class; at another stall Mrs Turton and her sisters; while Miss Barker and Mrs R. Barker, assisted by the Misses Hart, presided at another stall consisting chiefly of useful garments; Mr and Mrs Howgate, assisted by Mrs Ellerbeck, had the agricultural produce stall, kindly contributed by many of the farmers of the village, and also sent by Lady Sitwell. Mrs Kidd, Mrs Leng, Mrs De Taye, Mrs Carr, assisted by Mrs E. Kidd and the Misses Goodall, provided from the good things sent by the villagers an excellent afternoon tea, which was well patronised. Mr H. and Mr E. Rudgard presided over various amusements, such as cocoa-nut shy, bowls, &c., and Miss Hardcastle was very energetic in the sale of flowers.

PRESENTATION TO THE RETIRING VICAR. – The vicar of Scalby (Rev. W. Hesmondhalgh) and Mrs Hesmondhalgh have been presented with cheques for £100 and £23 respectively at a gathering of parishioners in the Scalby Parish Hall. The Rev. Hesmondhalgh is retiring after twenty-nine years as Vicar of Scalby [1944].

Mr A. Burgess presided, and recalled that during the vicariate of Mr Hesmondhalgh [1915–44] a new vicarage had been presented to the Church, the Parish Hall has been built, and the Schools have been enlarged. These would be a perpetual reminder of the work of the Vicar and Mrs Hesmondhalgh in their midst.

The Chairman presented the Vicar with the cheque for £100 which, he said, was made up of spontaneous gifts from many. Mrs Micklethwait presented Mrs Hesmondhalgh with a cheque for £23, and tributes were also paid by Mrs Verity, Mrs Bastiman, and Mr M.N. Lotinga ...

List of Incumbents

Date unknown	Walter/William		Reason not Known
14 Feb. 1238	Henry Devon	Brid[1]	By Death
16 Aug. 1254	Roger de Scarborough	Brid	
6 July 1319	William de Bessingby	Brid	By Death
1348	Robert de Sutton	Brid	For Living of Stillingfleet
23 May 1349	Richard de Wrelton	Brid	By Death
13 Oct. 1364	John Saylevur de Ulram	Brid	By Death
15 Dec. 1374	John, son of Adam de Burniston	Brid	For Living of Leathley
11 Jan. 1380	James de Cave	Brid	By Resignation
26 Mar. 1392	Robert Dalby	Brid	By Resignation
26 Apr. 1408	William de Hollym	Brid	For Chantry of Brampstone
18 Dec. 1409	Richard Lesset	Brid	
	Richard de Nafferton	Brid	By Resignation
28 July 1439	Henry Smith	Brid	
4 Dec. 1458	Henry Smith	Brid	By Death
10 Apr. 1480	William Greenhow	Brid	By Resignation
13 May 1501	William Ibson	Brid	
	Robert Storke	Brid	By Death
2 Oct. 1554	Henry Kay	Norwich[2]	By Resignation
22 July 1556	Richard Jenkinson	Norwich	By Resignation
3 Nov. 1576	Robert Wood	Norwich	By Resignation
16 May 1586	William de Buckton	Norwich	
14 June 1587	John Trowsdale	Farmer[3]	By Death
8 Feb. 1588	William Taylor	Farmer	By Death
6 July 1593	Thomas Bell	Farmer	By Death
13 Dec. 1621	George Harrison	H'son[4]	
21 Sept. 1623	*ad presentat*	Norwich	
23 June 1631	George Gay	Norwich	By Death
14 Aug. 1634	Nicholas Howlett		By Cession

20 Sept. 1662	Wm. Mompesson	Norwich	
1663	John Bosse	Norwich	
1690	Samuel Wilson	Norwich	By Death
1708	William Hollis	Norwich	By Death
8 Oct. 1737	William Ward, AB	Norwich	By Death
24 Apr. 1773	Thomas Preston, AM	Norwich	By Death
5 Aug. 1827	Chas. Augustus Thurlow	Norwich	By Resignation
12 July 1840	James Sedgewick, AM	Norwich	By Death
1870	James Bradbury Sweet, AM [for Barton-in-Fabis Rectory, Notts.]	Norwich	By Resignation
23 Nov. 1872	Lloyd Stewart Bruce, MA [Canon of York]	Norwich	By Appointment [to Carlton R., Notts.]
2 Feb. 1876	William Cautley Robinson	Norwich	By Resignation
1 Dec. 1915	William Hesmondhalgh, MA S. Cath. Coll. Cantab.	Norwich	By Resignation
29 Sept. 1944	Arthur Rowland Harry Grant, CVO, TD, MA, DD (Oxon) Chaplain to HM the King	Norwich	By Resignation Nov. 1949
July 1950	Edward Arthur Flowerday	Norwich	
24 Jan. 1959	Chris. Norman Tubbs, MA	Norwich	Still in Office

1. [Brid.] Prior & Convent of Bridlington Priory
2. [Norwich] Assigns of Dean & Chapter Norwich Cathedral
3. [Farmer] Assigns of Farmer of the Rectory
4. [H'son] John Harrison for this town [?Scarborough]

NOTES

1. Cole, J., *Historical Sketches of Scalby, Burniston & Cloughton*, 1829.
2. Hoveden, *Chron.* (YAS Rolls Series), i, 193.
3. Farrer, *Early Yorks Charters*, 282; *Cal. Pat.* 1345–48; Dugdale's *Monasticum* vi, 287; see also VCH.NR(i) 1914, p. 532.
4. *Cal. Pat.* 1345–48, p. 37.
5. *Archbishop Grey's Register*, p. 75 (Surtees Soc.).
6. Bacon's, *Liber Regis*.
7. *Cal. Pat.* I Edw. VI, Pt. iii, No. 35.
8. Inst. Bks (PRO).
9. *London Gazette*, 20 Oct. 1874.
10. Richardson, D.E., *A Brief History & Guide to Parish Church of St Laurence* (undated).
11. VCH.NR(ii) 1923.
12. Bulmer's *History & Directory of North Yorkshire*, 1890.
13. Poole, G.A. & Hugall, J.W., *The Churches of Scarborough, Filey and the Neighbourhood*, 1848.
14. Bulmer's op. cit., 1890.

15. Poole & Hugall, op. cit.
16. Richardson, op. cit.
17. VCH.NR(ii) 1923.
18. Ibid.
19. Poole & Hugall, op. cit.
20. Ibid.
21. VCH.NR(ii) 1923.
22. Richardson, op. cit.
23. Poole & Hugall, op. cit.
24. Ibid.
25. Ibid: a note in the parish register states that in 1767 'The gallery was repaired and a new staircase made into the same, and the whole painted.'
26. Ibid.
27. Richardson, op. cit.
28. Kelly's *Directory North Riding of Yorkshire*, 1905.
29. Charlton, L., *History of Whitby and of Whitby Abbey*, 1776.
30. Burton's *Monasticum*.
31. A somewhat exaggerated claim as the parish register shows that only 18 burials are recorded for 1625, compared with 19 in both 1624 and 1626, and 33 in 1623.
32. Cole, op. cit.
33. YAS Record Ser. Vol. LXXI (1927).
34. Cole, op. cit.
35. Kelly's, 1905.
36. Cole, op. cit.
37. YAS Record Ser. Vol. LXXI (1927).

CHAPTER FOUR

Village Tales

There is a time for everything,
and a season for every activity
under heaven:
a time to be born and a time to
    die,
a time to plant and a time to
    uproot,
a time to kill and a time to heal,
a time to tear down and a time to
    build,
a time to weep and a time to
    laugh,
a time to mourn and a time to
    dance . . .

Ecclesiastes 3:1–4 (NIV)

For the most, the countryman's life was an uneventful one. Measured and orderly, from birth to death, through season's change, it ground on. Only a few felt the hand of fame or notoriety. These left behind the substance of 'folklore' – provided the village tales – the rest, however, lived on in partial obscurity, playing, working, marrying and giving birth.

Today, people of a certain age living in the country speak of a remarkable and complete change in village life, far removed from the imagination of their children, grown up in a world of 'self-interest' and 'consumerism'. Some of these changes, like the loss of communal village life and the self-sufficiency of the village, came about slowly – almost imperceptibly – while others, like the revolution in agricultural practice, were surprisingly rapid. Traditions which grew through the centuries are now completely broken, due mainly to scientific advancement, especially in the field of transport and communications, and to higher educational standards.

Before the hectic pace and demands of the twentieth century, living was altogether simpler and cheaper, and family wants very modest – food, clothes, a roof over their heads, and perhaps a little bit for 'baccy and a treat for mother now and again. A saying of the fathers of that day was: 'Save up until you can afford it, and by the time you've saved enough you'll find you don't want it.'

Saving was almost a religion, and was for many a real necessity. Almost every child had a 'trip-box' and when he was given a penny or two for running an errand or such, the gift was generally accompanied by the advice: 'Don't spend it, save it.' There was a farm worker at Scalby Nabs whose ambition was to save £100 and take a small farm of his

A typical cottage or farm garden at Scalby with hens and chicks running 'free'. The garden was a necessity for many a humble cottager who used the land to grow food for the table to supplement his poor wages

own. In spite of the meagre wages of his day, he succeeded in doing this while comparatively young. Most families paid weekly contributions into the 'club' for clothes or extra 'tit-bits' at Christmas, and to a Friendly Society for old age or death.

Sometimes, however, the Yorkshireman's frugality was carried to extremes. On one occasion at the local vestry meeting somebody complained about the only pen being badly corroded and suggested a new nib might be provided. Another member, who was well known for his aversion to spending money, said: 'Nay, there's no need for that. I'll just scrat it up a bit with my penknife and it'll last for years yet.'

There were many ways of supplementing a small income. Every cottage had a garden where vegetables and fruit were grown, and in addition an allotment was often cultivated. Livestock was kept where there was suitable accommodation. Cows, poultry, bees, pigeons and rabbits all contributed to the household coffers as well as the larder. But the cottager's best friend was the pig. It could be fed economically from table scraps and the like, and usually would be fattened for eventual home curing; a breeding sow was no bad investment, evidenced by an account given by Gilbert White, of Selbourne, who wrote in his famous *Natural History*, when trying to determine the life-span of pigs, how he did discover one old sow some sixteen or seventeen years of age 'who was as thick as she was long, and whose belly swept on the ground'.

> For about ten years this prolific mother produced two litters in the year of about ten at a time, and once above twenty in a litter. From long experience in the world this female was grown very sagacious and artful. When she found occasion to converse [mate] with a boar, she used to open all the intervening gates, and march, by herself,

up to a distant farm where one was kept; and when her purpose was served she would return by the same means. She proved, when killed, good bacon, juicy and tender; the rind or sward was remarkably thin. At a moderate computation she was allowed to have been the fruitful parent of three hundred pigs. She was killed in spring, 1775.[1]

Hereabouts at Scalby, among the village festivals and festivities, 'pig-killing' was still celebrated for many years beyond its original derivation. This seems to have been a survival of the old custom of killing off and salting down all livestock that was not to be kept for breeding or working. And so each autumn the pig-killing continued. This was an important occasion, because, as we have noted, home-cured hams and bacon formed a great part of the countryman's diet. The slaughter was followed by a supper to which friends and neighbours were invited, and there was much rejoicing. In turn, throughout that season, cottagers would be invited to other 'pig-killings'.

Self-sufficiency, in many cases, meant farming. The farm produced most commodities for the village community – corn for grinding locally, silk, eggs and more, including employment for the men, and at busy periods or harvest-time, extra employment for the children and housewives.

The novice at farming at the turn of the century was not bound as an apprentice, as a tradesman would have been, but was 'hired' under a yearly contract. At Martinmas [11 November] the farm-hands were paid off and given a week's holiday.

At the beginning of this century a youngster would get between £7 and £9 for his first year's work as a 'bullocky' or 'thoddy'. As he became more knowledgeable his status increased and, as 'wag', he would receive about £18. A foreman would receive a little more.

The young farm labourer's ambition was to become a 'wag' or wagoner, responsible for his team of two, three or four horses. He then took great pride in the condition and appearance of these animals. Nothing gave him greater pleasure than a favourable remark about his team. Hence the tactful approach of the scrounger or tramp: 'Noo, wag, thi 'osses looks fat. 'As tha got a bit o' 'bacca?'

An old horse became very knowing and competent in all its work, and it was customary to yoke a young and frisky one with an older and sedate one, so that it could learn by example. On one occasion, when a very young boy was trying his hand at harrowing a field, a person watching remarked to the farmer that it seemed incongruous that such a frail little chap should be in charge of such a huge shire horse. The farmer replied indignantly: 'You don't imagine he's sent there to teach the old mare to harrow, do you? She's teaching him.'

During Martinmas week the farm worker had to visit the market town (in this case Scarborough). He had to renew his wardrobe, for there would be little chance of doing so later for want of free time. The regulation dress was pale-coloured corduroy with slightly bell-bottomed trousers. During the holiday week, sparkle was added by adorning the hat and coat lapels with cheap and gaudy celluloid ornaments. The worker was now a free man and unless he were 'stopping on' he must get hired to another master. This done he received his 'fest [feast] money' which, like the 'king's shilling' to the soldier, sealed his fate – at least for another year.

It was usual for all the unmarried hands on a farm to live in the farmhouse. Discipline was strict and behaviour correct under the farm foreman. Social status of each grade in the

Foulsyke Farm, Scalby, showing the entrance to
the farmyard with a dovecote in the tower

farm community was rigorously observed. Thus it was not only unmannerly but almost a
crime to address anyone in a higher circle than oneself in the familiar second person.
When a young farm-hand, newly arrived on a farm, inadvertently addressed the foreman
as 'thoo' (thou), the latter exclaimed witheringly: 'What, thoo, thooing me? Thoo has nay
right to thoo nobody, thoo hasn't.'

Corn was hand sown, a man going ahead making holes with a dibber and the children
following behind placing five grains in each hole and chanting a rhyme, one of many
similar:

> One for the blackbird,
> One for the crow,
> Two for the devil,
> And one to grow.

Reaping was done by hand with the scythe, younger people following the reapers to
'mak ban's' by twisting two handfuls of straw together with which they bound the
sheaves. The horse-drawn reaper and later, self-binder, eliminated all this toil.

One of the earliest mechanical labour-saving devices on the farm was the threshing
machine – cumbersome but efficient. In its time this was both drawn and driven by a
sturdily built traction-engine powered by coal and steam. Imagine the traction-engine and

threshing machine leaving Prospect Farm ('Quaker' Smithson's), going along the unmade Carr Lane and then, with a man carrying a red flag in front, making its way along deeply rutted lanes to, say, Scalby Nabs. Only the stoutest machines could ever have survived such a journey.

In spite of the hard work and loneliness, there was never any lack of recruits for farming, and workers took a great pride in the skills they acquired and the livestock they tended. No doubt the quality and quantity of food supplied on a typical farm compensated for many inconveniences. The first question a new hand asked about the farm was: 'What sort of meat spot is it?' And the highest recommendation one could give was: 'Oh, it's very fair; knife and fork three times a day.' One youth, eulogizing the farm he had chosen to work at, finished by exclaiming: 'Why, even the bacon-cake's made with ham.'

It was not only the men who worked long hours – the housewife had quite a day of it. In addition to the ordinary household chores, she was responsible for the butter churning and brewing, and the making of mead from honey and wines from flowers, fruits or roots. Then she prepared all the necessary preserves, pickles and jams; after that, there was the weekly household baking. There were no gas or electric ovens, but one could do a day's baking more easily and without contracting backache, for the built-in oven was almost breast-high, and even the fire underneath it was usually some two feet above floor level. Many of the Victorian ovens remain in Scalby, even if they are not in use. One survives in the old part of Church Beck House.

In still older houses it is possible to find brick bread-ovens. These were just a square cavity in the wall with a flue at the furthest end, suitably lined with fire-brick. A wood fire was lit inside the oven, and kept burning while the dough was rising on the hearth nearby. When all was ready, the fire was raked out and the loaves thrust inside the hot oven to bake.

Such was the importance of bread in the diet up to that time, in case anyone did not have such amenities as an oven, public bakeries were common, and one existed in Scalby, first mentioned in 1313–14 and again in 1322.[2] It stood on the Waste of Burniston.[3] A tale is told of one occasion, when a housewife went to fetch the 'meat-and-taty pie' she had taken earlier to the bake-house, only the crust remained, the pie filling filched, whereon she composed this grace:

> O Lord my God send down the word
> With rusty swords and sickles
> To cut the throats of all those folks
> That's eaten up my vittles.

When roads were bad and transport poor, it was essential that as much work as possible was undertaken by the village craftsmen, and frequently one man would be skilled in more than his trade. Scalby, for instance, had three 'smithies', even when the population was less than one thousand inhabitants. In South Street Mr W. Coultas and Mr R. Boddy had their smithies, facing each other, and Mr J.G. Boddy carried on a similar business in North Street. The first of these ceased operation in the late nineteenth century; the other two, being carried on by sons in each case, continued until the 1960s.

The village blacksmith had to be a very versatile man. Apart from making and repairing farm implements and, of course, shoeing horses, he was expected to be something of a locksmith, whitesmith and tinsmith. He would make to order anything from a pair of wrought-iron gates to a child's play hoop. Tool-making was not excluded, and it is told how an old resident, chopping down a tree, stopped to admire his axe and was heard to say: 'It is an old axe, but it is the best one ever I had; J.G. Boddy forged it for me.'

Still more surprising is the story of a local smith during the Second World War. In desperation, unable to get any shoeing-iron for horses, he took a couple of old ploughshares, beat them into bars, and from them turned out a set of shoes. Commenting on the feat, the smith concerned added ruefully that this practice was not a paying proposition, as the shoes took too long in the making and, when made, outlasted three ordinary sets.

The fate of the village carpenter was possibly happier than that of his neighbour, the blacksmith, for his skill remained in demand long after, and is still sought today. Some ninety years ago there were three carpentry works in the village. Mr Edwin Beacroft, who, it is said, was responsible for the whole of the interior of the late North Street chapel when it was redesigned before demolition years after, emigrated to California. Then there was Mr John Gibson, who had a place that later became known as Grove Works, and whose son and later his grandson, kept on the business at Church Becks.

The son, Mr Thomas Gibson, was always interested in woodcarving, and his handiwork can be seen in the lettering on the Queen Victoria memorial seat at Cumboots, and the Coronation seat near the Rosette Inn.

Originally known as Scalby Low Mill, a water corn-mill, it was often damaged by flooding and choked by 'the immense quantity of debris including trees, broken bridges, dead pigs &c' brought downstream by the waters. It suffered a fire in 1821. By 1850 the main building had become a hotel and was popular as a 'Strawberry Tea Garden'. The hotel catered for all tastes and the low single-storey building on the left was a 'Temperance Refreshment Room'. Cole recalls in 1820 that 'recently a remarkably fine specimen of a fossil tooth of an Asiatic Elephant was found on these sands, near Scalby Mill'

Scalby Mills Hotel, with visitors from Scarborough seeking the quieter aspects of the district and enjoying the donkeys

Working hours were long; there was no machinery. Even matchboarding had to be tongue and grooved using handplanes. Every carpenter was an expert in the use of the adze – a tool that is quite superfluous today. Yet John Gibson, it is said, could make a pair of oak gateposts in a remarkably short time, using no other tool. And, when finished, all faces were quite square and true.

Some other old occupations (though enjoying a revival in certain areas today) have disappeared entirely. There are now no thatchers; dry-stone wallers are as scarce as corncrakes; and brewing and milling are no longer carried on as a one-man undertaking, though the latter survived in some measure until the 1950s in Scalby.

Scalby never possessed a windmill, although Scarborough had at least two and there was the conspicuous one at the Peak, Ravenscar. But this deficiency was made up for by several water-driven mills. The earliest recorded was one belonging to the Crown in 1164 worth £6.[4] In February 1609, the Crown alienated the two water-mills of Scalby, the water-mill at Longdale End on Scalby Beck, and a fishery going to Edward Ferrers and Francis Phelips.[5] Arthur Rowntree, relative of J.W. Rowntree, writing in his *History of Scarborough*, mentions the handing down through the years of a mill on Scalby Beck in the ownership of the Lacey family which was probably High Mill situated above Scalby Bridge Mill: 'Robert Lacie leaves a mylne at Scalby Beck in 1607, John Lacey leaves one watermylne in 1623 and Robert Lacie one watter milne in Scawbie Beck called the Upper Water in 1628.'

What is now known as Scalby Mills was formerly Scalby Low Mill. It frequently suffered damage from high seas, and had to give up the struggle against the elements when destroyed by fire. However, it was still in operation as late as 1840, when the miller

Between Newby Bridge and the sea at Scalby Mill, a distance of about 1½ miles, there were four water-powered corn-mills. Top picture shows Newby Mill (left) and Scalby Bridge Mill (just visible) on either side of Scalby Beck Bridge on the Burniston Coastal Road. Scalby Bridge Mill (bottom picture) became a Youth Hostel, while Newby Mill (top) was demolished

was recorded as Joseph Robinson.[6] In 1829 Cole, in discussing the course of the 'Cut' at Scalby, states, 'the proposed course of the river would pass the mills above the Whitby Road. Below is a mill in disuse, and one in good repair close to the sea, near to which the vale on both sides is bounded by rocks'. He goes on to say:

> In the garden of this retreat, appear several neat edifices, erected for the purpose of displaying the tea-equipage during the summer months, round which grow pendent laburnums and honey-suckles, this spot being much frequented in the Scarborough season by parties formed for the purpose of taking tea, amid the charms of rural scenery. . . . From a rustic seat at the top of one of the eminences which serve to encircle this rural and romantic scene, we gain a bird's-eye view of the mill, and its small plot of garden ground.[7]

Scalby High Mill – High Mill Farm in 1957 – was conveniently erected where the Cowath Beck joined the old Scalby Beck. Mr Archer Wilkinson left the Rosette Inn by 1872[8] to take charge of this mill and it was still recorded as being in his ownership in 1890.' The mill was taken over by his son Edwin, before he decided to give his full time to farming at Scalby Nabs. In later years Scalby High Mill became a Youth Hostel.

The last of the water-mills to work was Newby Mill, which stood just below the bridge on Burniston Road. It was demolished by the 1950s, but many people remember seeing the water-wheel, even after it ceased to operate as a working mill about the time of the First World War.

The last working millers were the Flintons, Tom and his sons William 'Bill' (recorded as miller in 1855[10]) and his brother Israel, both expert in 'dressing' millstones which had to be tended as they wore smooth. Stone for millstones was originally quarried on Cloughton Moor.[11] Not only did the Flintons produce millstones for their own mill, but undertook similar work for the few surviving mills in the surrounding district. Later, they found their task made more difficult with imported French stones (probably granite) which were used for flour-making. This stone proved almost as hard as the chisel used to cut it.

It was not very long ago that the stone-breaker was to be seen on every county road. Heaps of hard stone were tipped in readiness at convenient distances along the verges of the road, and it was the duty of the stone-breaker to reduce the huge lumps to 'nuts' of a suitable size. He arrived in the morning bringing a sack for kneeling on, his hammer, a bundle of spare hazel hammer shafts and his wire-gauze spectacles to protect his eyes from stray chips. Throughout the day the familiar tap-tap could be heard as he followed his monotonous job. His wage was low, about 18s. a week.

Until well into this century, there was no good road connection between Scalby and Hackness. Presumably wagons would have to make their way from Suffield Heights (seat of Sir Posthumous Hoby, lord of the manor of Hackness) to Swinesdale Farm and through Scalby Nabs. But in about 1800 Sir Vanden Bempde Johnstone built the new road from Suffield 'at about £600 expense'.

One occupation that will never see the light of day again, was 'coo-tenting'. Each morning the 'coo-tenter' (meaning cow tender) made his round of the village collecting the cottager's cows. It is said Ernest Franklin, when engaged on this job, carried a small horn in his pocket, the blowing of which gave warning of his approach, and the cows were turned out to join his growing herd. When all had been collected, they were driven to some lane or road and left to graze the grassy verge with minimum supervision until time for evening milking, when they would be returned.

Country folk were self-reliant in many other ways too, most had a good knowledge of the uses of medicinal herbs and simple remedies, both for human ailments and their livestock. Doctors were few and far between and expensive, and became commonplace only towards the nineteenth century. Nobody bothered about how and why certain flowers, fruits, leaves or roots had beneficial effects and while for many years these simple cures have been frowned upon, they worked. Today there is a tendency to revive them in our wisdom!

When two little boys disturbed a wasp's nest with the inevitable result, their mother, at her wit's end as to what to do, sent for a neighbour who knew all the old treatments. She took a spadeful of damp earth and pressed a handful wherever there were signs of a sting, and in a few minutes all pain had gone.

A young man, very consumptive, was advised by his doctor to get away from the smoke and fog of his own town into the country, preferably near the sea, and he came to a farm in Scalby. Old Sammy, who though illiterate was wise in country lore, made this pale-faced, weedy, coughing youth follow him as he ploughed. Every now and again he instructed the young man to grasp a handful of earth and 'sniff at it', and that was all. Asked how this could cure anybody, Sammy explained: 'Newly turned earth contains a lot of oxygen, and by breathing this in a few hours a day it did him good.'

The first medical man recorded in the district was George Peckett Dale in 1872,[12] his address and occupation being given as surgeon, Haybrow. He was still practising in 1890.[13]

By the end of the decade, the centre of medicine had moved to Cloughton, and took in the outlying districts of Newby, Throxenby, Burniston, Hayburn Wyke, Staintondale, Ravenscar, Harwood Dale and included Scalby. This 'round' was undertaken by Dr Wilkinson on horseback. Dr B.G. Foreman took over his practice in 1902 and made his calls by motor car – a hazardous undertaking in itself considering the indifferent state of the roads at that period.

There was no ambulance service nor local hospital either, and a doctor had to be prepared to operate in awkward places. On one occasion, it is said, when there had been a wreck on the coast, two or three of the villagers thought it might be profitable to pay it a visit after dark. Unfortunately, one had the misfortune to fall down the cliff to the rocks below. Dr Malvin, who had the surgery then, was summoned; in the meantime, the casualty was carried on a door to the nearest house. In addition to numerous broken bones, he was bleeding badly and something had to be done quickly to stop his life ebbing away; so the doctor called on two of the 'stretcher' party and showed them how to control the flow of blood, saying: 'Hang on till I tell you to relax. The man's life depends on it.' For what must have seemed an eternity these unwilling helpers watched the gory proceedings in silence, until at last the doctor said to let go. Immediately there were two heavy thuds as his assistants slid to the floor in a faint!

When villagers were more or less isolated, the inhabitants had to make their own amusement. In summer, working hours extended into the late evening, and any free time there was would be devoted to outdoor sports. But the winter nights were long and afforded ample time for improvised entertainment. People tended to be more musical (or less reticent) than they are now, for players and singers were always forthcoming. The village supported a Women's Choir, who were often mentioned as winners of one competition or another. They took two cups at the Eskdale Tournament of Song in 1951; won the Adela Shaw Cup for Advanced Choirs, and the Dorothy Pennyman Cup at the WI Festival at York in 1954; and they were awarded the John Smith Rose Bowl in the open class for Women's Choirs at the Keighley Music Festival. Most of these were won under the conductorship of Miss M. Dowson, with J. Riley mentioned as accompanist, and it is noted that the name of Miss Kidd features among those picked out for special consideration many times. The songs were usually very comic, sentimental or fell into the category of 'old standards' – the folk songs of the 1880s.

At Christmas-time the 'Mummers' did the round of Scalby, giving their performance inside each house in turn. This old custom died out about the end of the last century; although sporadic attempts were made to revive it up until the late 1950s, few people showed interest and it was doubted whether anyone could remember the characters at that time (Beelzebub included) or the dialogue.

Barn dances were at one time very popular and still persist in many villages. When the school was built, it became the centre of social life. The children who had attended it during the day for instruction returned in the evening for amusement, and their parents, who had at one time been pupils, came back for instruction or entertainment.

Before motor transport was known, a great day in every youngster's life was the annual Sunday school treat. This event needed a good deal of preparation, and everyone 'mucked in'. Several farm wagons had to be borrowed from willing farmers, so the date had to be fixed outside of hay-time and harvest. The wagons were then thoroughly cleaned and washed, sometimes even repainted. The traditional colours were oxide red for wheels, undercarriage and shafts, picked out with lines of white or black; stone-colour for the body, lined with green, blue or red, or all three; and black for the iron fittings. To make the interior more comfortable for the children, the long curved boards overhanging the wheels, which ran each side of the wagon, were upholstered with bags of chaff or hay. The cart floor was littered deep in straw.

The horses gave each wagoner an opportunity to display his skill and imagination in decoration. The animals themselves were curry-combed and brushed until they shone and gleamed all over; the harness was cleaned with leather-soap and all metal, including the numerous horse-brasses, was made to shine. Steel chains were dropped into a bag half-full of dry sharp sand, which was suspended so as to touch lightly the wheel of some vehicle that, when revolved, scoured the metal links till they shone like silver.

All this was just routine. The skill and artistic ability of the wagoner were exemplified in the decoration of his team with coloured ribbon, rosettes and whatever he fancied. As the normal farm work had to go on uninterrupted, most of the cleaning and preparation had to be undertaken after working hours, probably by candlelight.

Then came the day. The wagons assembled at about nine o'clock on the appointed morning, and the excited children, decked out in their Sunday best, scrambled aboard. Then began the long, slow, jolting journey to the seaside. A lunch of beef sandwiches and lemonade was taken, and the young were then free to spend their afternoon and their 'trip money' as they pleased.

Concerts were very popular, and in the minutes of the old Reading-Room there are frequent references to the school borrowing seats from it (or vice versa) for the holding of an entertainment. And in the Kidd journal, a newspaper cutting recalls just such an event:

A public tea was held in the Reading-Room on Tuesday week, when a large number partook of the good things which had been provided for them. The trays were presided over by Mrs Cooke, Mrs Brown, Miss Green, and others. After tea a concert was given by several friends out of the village and from Scarborough, to a crowded house. The performers were deservedly applauded for their rendering of the different pieces, encores being very frequent, the songs by Miss Hodgson, and the songs in the second part by Mr C. Leng and Mr J. Hampton being especially good. Miss Hampton, Miss Cooke, and Mrs Spurr presided at the pianoforte. Mr Bailey, of Scarborough, created considerable amusement during the interval by his thought-reading entertainment. Mr Cooke proposed a vote of thanks to the ladies who presided over the trays, and to the various performers, to which Mr Bailey responded.

Lectures, on a great variety of subjects, were well attended too, especially when illustrated by the 'magic lantern'. Although Education Authorities did not concern themselves with evening institutes as they do today, some further education was carried on by private enterprise. The women of the village played a part in organizing these activities. Miss Cooke, who lived at the Holt, was an accomplished wood-carver and gave instruction in this craft, and Miss Nelson, an assistant teacher at the old National School, taught cane basketry. An instructor from the artillery barracks ran a course in physical education, and we can see from a newspaper account that the winter first-aid course, held in the Temperance Hall, was a resounding success:

A very interesting meeting took place in the Temperance Hall, Scalby, on Wednesday week, the occasion being the distribution of certificates to those members of the Ambulance Classes (which have recently been held in the village) who successfully passed the recent examination in: 'First Aid to the Injured'. The chair was taken by Mr J.E. Ellis, MP, who first called upon Mr Tickle, Hon. Secretary to the Corps, to read the report, which stated that out of 38 members of the classes who were examined on the 31st January, by Surgeon-Major Hutton, organising commissioner of the St John's Ambulance Association, 37 successfully passed the examination. Several members of the men's class then went through the various drills, illustrative of the methods of bandaging, carrying out by stretcher and by hand, lifting etc. the evolutions being very creditably performed; after which Mr Ellis presented the certificates . . . among which is the name of Henry Kidd . . . Mr Ellis then called upon Mr Tickle to make a presentation to the lecturer Dr D.R. Chambers, of Scarborough, who had most kindly conducted the classes gratuitously throughout the winter. The testimonial, which was subscribed for by all those attending the lectures, was a handsomely fitted travelling bag . . . Mrs J.A. Cooke then presented from the Ladies' Committee four volumes of organ music, to Mr Tickle, who had been throughout a most able and energetic secretary. . . . [It was understood] that the names of those qualified to render 'First Aid' in case of accident will be posted in conspicuous position in the village, so that in case of need their services may be requisitioned.

Visits of the Church Army should not, perhaps, be classed as entertainment, but they certainly afforded interest and enjoyment. The Army in this case consisted only of Captain

Nye, Lieutenant Coleman and the very likeable Brother Patrick (who did all the chores and spade-work and sang hymns at the same time).

Arriving in their horse-drawn caravan, they would set up camp in Mr Vernon's field and then get on with their evangelical work. They could be sure of filling the schoolroom nightly. The young came to see the 'magic lantern' slides, the village maidens to view the strangers, and the rest of Scalby to let their hearts rejoice in the boisterous singing of those good old Sankey and Moody hymns, of which the words and tunes were so easily memorized.

The English concertina was a very popular instrument in those nineteenth-century days, and many a barn dance, country dance or sword dance had no other accompaniment than the concertina, though the fiddle was its rival. Handbell ringing was at one time popular, and Scalby had a team of ringers that saw a decline at the beginning of the century, but which has seen a revival in latter years.

Musical entertainment was not, however, all supplied locally. Occasionally a German band made its appearance. Also, on account of its nearness to Scarborough, the village was able to enjoy musical entertainment that was denied the more distant parishes. Italian organ-grinders were regular visitors too, and their names became familiar.

When the piano-organ ousted the older types of musical entertainment, the intimacy of the old organ-grinder was lost. No longer was it necessary to visit every backyard individually, for the notes of the new instrument were sufficiently powerful to reach a whole group of houses at once, and while one man turned the handle his companion could go round collecting the pennies!

It was not only music that Italians had to offer. They kept the villagers, especially the children, supplied with ice-cream. This was brought round in little gaily painted pony-drawn carts. No outdoor gathering was complete without its ice-cream cart and the familiar cry of 'Okey-pokey-penny-a-lump'.

Possibly the biggest 'social' event of the calendar was Scalby Sports Day, held, by tradition, on old Midsummer Day. This was essentially a holiday for everybody, old and young alike. The sports followed the usual country programme. Cole referred to this custom, writing:

> Old Midsummer-day is, at Scalby, a kind of gala time, when 'The Sports', as they are termed, take place, consisting of the most rustic description of amusements, such as Donkey-racing, &c. and when Booths are erected for the accommodation of the several visitors, and the village presents a motley fair-like appearance.
>
> The celebration of 'The Sports' of the different villages in the county of York has probably arisen from the dedication of the church, and these sports are most likely a corruption of 'The Wake' of the midland counties. We say corruption, for there, the design of its original institution is not forgotten; as, on the Sunday throngs of visitants from the neighbouring villages repair to attend the afternoon service of the church, when sermons, tending to correct immorality and disorder are delivered.[14]

These sports were last held in 1861. But the sports did not die out so much as merge with the local show, and in recent years all the usual booths and amusements were to be found in Scalby on showday, presenting all the features of a village fair; and in latter years

'Scalby Fair', as it has now come to be known in its revival, in spirit, enshrines the old 'sports' and later Horticultural Show that filled the mid-June weeks.

Before 1886 Cloughton, Burniston and Scalby Floral and Horticultural Society held shows in the three villages in rotation. But in that year Scalby decided to 'go it alone', and thus held a show each August ever since with the exception of the 1914–18 and 1939–45 war years. The first president was Major Brockwell, of Church Beck House, and among the patrons were Sir George Sitwell, the Hon. Capt. Johnstone, Col. Steble and Mr Ernest Beckett, MP – all people with strong Scalby connections through past or present residency.

Newspaper cuttings pasted into the Kidd album record with pride the family contributions to these shows, and in reproducing two illustrate the vitality and affection with which the annual show was held by the village. It is noted that Henry Kidd took a prize for a dressed fowl in the 'cottagers only' class, and another in the 'cottagers and farmers', while the ladies of the family distinguished themselves in patchwork and cot quilting (Mrs Kidd); needlework (Frances Kidd); and in knitting (Milly Kidd), often in more than one class:

The second annual show of the Scalby Floral and Horticultural Society was held on Wednesday at Scalby, near Scarborough. Glorious weather prevailed, and the attendance was very good. The entries were exhibited in two spacious marquees erected in a field near to the schoolhouse. The number of the exhibits and their general quality were much in excess of last year's show, and the prize money offered was over £25. The judges committee sat down to luncheon at the Nag's Head Inn, when the President (Mr Cooke) occupied the chair. The third annual exhibition of needlework, quilting, and patchwork in connection with the Scalby and Burniston Industrial Society was held also at Scalby on Wednesday. The arrangements were admirably carried out by the committee, viz., Mrs Green, Mrs Cooke, Miss Barker, and Mrs Wharton. There was a good number of exhibits, which shows that a great interest is taken in the working of the Society. The weather was fine but as the flower show was being held in the village at the same time, somewhat mitigated against attendance. Some excellent hand-painted china was kindly lent by Miss Cooke. The same kindly interest was taken in the work of the Society by Mrs Rugards, who sent some exquisite Turkish drapery as well as paintings. The cottagers seem to have been greatly benefited by the efforts of the Society for some excellent patchwork and knitted hearthrugs were shown, while the sewing was very neat and tidy. In the children's class everything showed a marked improvement.

On Tuesday afternoon the Cloughton, Burniston, Scalby, and District Floral, Horticultural, and Industrial Society held its ninth annual show at Scalby, in a couple of large tents pitched in a field belonging to Dr Jones, and but for the rather treacherous character of the weather it would have proved a complete success. So far as exhibits were concerned there was nothing left to be desired either in the open or the cottagers' classes, both coming out strong in vegetables, and the flower department of both was above average excellence. Agriculture was also well represented in all classes of cereal produce. The farmers' wives and daughters had been especially industrious in the preparation of samples of their skill in churning, and the result was the large number of 42 baskets of butter. . . . In addition to the show above mentioned, there was held in connection with it the second annual Industrial Exhibition in the school, and we have no hesitation in saying that the examples shown of quilts, needlework, &c., were unexceptionally good, and rarely, if ever, surpassed in any local show. The people of Scalby and adjacent villages mustered pretty strongly, and, notwithstanding the squally weather, there was a fair contingent from Scarborough by train and otherwise. The Scalby brass band played a variety of music during the day. . . . In the course of the day a luncheon took place at the Nag's Head Inn, Mr W. Ward, the President of the society, occupying the chair, and Mr C. Leadley, one of the vice-presidents, the vice-chair. After the loyal toasts the secretary (Mr Wiley) proposed the health of the patrons, coupling with the toast the name of Mr J.E. Ellis (Wrea Head), who responded, and concluded by proposing 'The Judges' – The President responded for the lady judges, and Mr C. Leadley for himself and gentlemen colleagues. The health of the President and other officers were also drank, and they were warmly thanked for their services . . .

A final step was the amalgamation of the floral show and the foal show. It is difficult to determine when the foal show started. Possibly it grew out of the declining cattle market, which at one period in history was of considerable importance.

Gordon Home in his *Evolution of an English Town*, gives a list of local cattle marks used in our markets some three hundred years ago. The mark indicating *Scalbi* and *Scalbi Haye* was, in both instances, a crude letter H. A small-scale cattle mart continued to be held in the Nag's Head Yard until the beginning of the present century.

If cattle marts and fairs were not to the villagers' taste, there was always drama, and the dramatic group of the Scalby Women's Institute was most accomplished according to an account in the press following an appearance in York (10 May) in the Drama Festival of the Yorkshire County Federation of Women's Institutes:

They entered the novice section and gained 90 per cent and the play presented was 'March Wedding' by Muriel and Sydney Box. The adjudicator, Miss Gwen Latty awarded them a First Class Certificate and commented very favourably on the production and acting, mentioning in particular the beautiful and controlled performance of Mary Mitchelson, who played the part of the bride. The adjudicator expressed appreciation of the setting of the stage and congratulated the team on a sincere and well-balanced performance. The players were as follows: Mary Mitchelson, Muriel Tickle, Doreen Robinson, Mildred Kidd, Olive Parkinson, Gladys Defty, Sylvia Rines, Margaret Turner and Phoebe Taylor.

Another cutting, dated 1928, recalls that much of the dramatic entertainment was put on as fund-raising for various causes – for instance, the Scalby Area Bed Endowment Fund for the Scarborough New Hospital; or in aid of the National Institute for the Blind:

This group of players [Scalby Amateur Players] have made three previous appearances in Scalby, Cloughton, and Scarborough, and their fourth concert was well patronised, the Hall [Parish Hall] being well filled.

A large part of the programme was occupied by two one-act plays. The first, 'The Perfect Butler', dealt with the changed conditions since the war, showing a young man of excellent connections as butler to one of the new rich. Naturally he knew exactly what the perfect butler should be like, but he was not quite perfection, and when his wife, who had taken a situation in a shop, came on a secret visit there were interesting and amusing complications.

Mr L. Raine caused a good deal of fun as the butler, and was well supported by Mrs McKinley as his wife, Miss M. Coultas as the mistress, and Mr J. Newlove, the master.

The other play 'Escape', presented a scene in a Dartmoor cottage on a misty night when two convicts had escaped from the prison. One of the convicts eventually arrives at the cottage, which is really the house of his wife. She has made all preparations for his flight from the country and this is about to take place when the police arrive. Will the disguise of the convict be discovered or not is the interesting problem which keeps the audience in suspense. Mr P. Knowles succeeded excellently in portraying the hopes and fears of a man who has just escaped from the horrors of prison. The part of his anxious wife was creditably taken by Miss M. Kidd. Other parts of a friend, Miss E. Newlove, and a sergeant of police, Mr H. Newlove, were well sustained.

The rest of the programme, every item of which was greatly enjoyed, was: Opening chorus, 'Hello!'; sea shanty, 'Billy Boy' and 'Rio Grande'; song, Miss Newlove; duet, Miss Brown and Mr Knowles; concerted 'Chump Chop'; song, G. Bastiman; shanty, 'Shenandoah'; trio, 'Spinsters Three'; song, D. Ward; duet, Misses Brown and Coultas; concerted, 'In the beautiful bye and bye'. Mr P. Beedle was the very able accompanist, and the secretary for the effort was Mr L. Raine.

Mr Halliday Huggan proposed a vote of thanks to the players for their work on behalf of the blind and to the audience for their support.

Mildred Kidd was an enthusiastic thespian, and took part in a number of productions by the Scalby Players and the Scalby Girls' Club. In the latter, taking the role of Lady Elmsdale in a play entitled *A Modern Cinderella*.

By contrast, other pleasures and pastimes indulged in by the inhabitants of Scalby were not so innocent. There was a brief time when the district boasted a 'house of ill-repute':

In the middle of August 1924, two seemingly 'genteel' ladies rented a house at Scalby. The property – named 'The Cottage', and recently occupied by Henry Marsden – was situated just beyond the village on Burniston Road.

Local gossips with a knack of nosing out secrets soon discovered that the two strangers were Ann Galloway (81), of Somerscales Street, Hull, and Eliza Pearson (72), of Hopwood Street, Hull, who had been advised by their doctor to have a long holiday in the country. They had rented the fully-furnished cottage for six weeks at a weekly rent of £2 12s 6d.

Sharp-eyed locals quickly noticed that an exceptionally large number of visitors called at the cottage each evening. Such people tended to be rather common young women and smartly-dressed men who arrived by taxi and often stayed the night.

Suspecting that the cottage's tenants might be 'flash ladies' rather than 'genteel ladies', several of Scalby's 'moral watchdogs' voiced their suspicions to the local chief of police, Inspector Letty. He promptly organised a nightly surveillance on the property, beginning Monday, September 1st.

That evening – armed with binoculars – Inspector Letty and two police-constables hid in the cottage garden. At 11 pm they saw a two-seater motor car containing two men, park on the cottage driveway. Once the men had entered the cottage Inspector Letty noted the car's number. Then he and his colleagues turned their attention to the bedroom windows. Before long, through a space in the curtains of the north bedroom, they witnessed a man and woman undress each other and then climb into bed. Thereafter, the couple's activities were invisible to the police prying eyes!

Next evening, at about 11.45 pm, the same car and a taxi arrived at the cottage. Several men, two women and the taxi driver made a noisy entry through the front door. At 12.45 am – through gaps in the bedroom curtains – the police saw men and women, in a state of undress, climb in and out of beds.

For the next four nights the policemen watched the cottage and recorded details of its nocturnal visitors. At 11 pm on September 6th, three men and two women arrived by taxi and took crates of bottles into the cottage. When the men left about 11.45 pm, one was heard to say: 'They're a rum lot in there'. At 12.50 am more people arrived by taxi and within five minutes, the police noticed 'a man and woman in each of the bedrooms and another couple in the sitting room'. But what exactly they were doing was not clearly visible through the thin, fully-drawn curtains!

The police's nightly vigil continued for nine days, during which time men and women were observed 'arriving at the cottage and undressing in its bedrooms'. Inspector Letty, who devoted numerous hours to the operation, was firmly convinced that the cottage was 'a house of ill-repute' which warranted an inspection.

On September 10th, at 11.30 pm, the policemen watched a taxi bring two men and two women to the cottage. One of the men told the taxi driver: 'You'd better come back about 8.15 tomorrow morning'. It was obvious to Inspector Letty that an all-night session was planned by the revellers – an ideal time for a police raid!

Determined to catch their 'birds in the nest', the police did not enter the cottage until about 1.00 am. Finding no one in the ground floor rooms, they crept upstairs as quietly as they could while wearing hobnailed boots. Bursting into the north bedroom, they were disappointed to find two beds with a man in each, but no sign of any women!

Inspector Letty invaded the other bedroom where he found Anne Galloway, Eliza Pearson and a naked young woman huddled together in a double bed. A search revealed another young woman, clad only in a transparent nightdress, hiding in the lavatory.

Intimidated by the brusque policemen, the two men made a statement admitting, 'They had picked up the two girls at a hotel bar in Scarborough and accompanied them to the cottage for a night of immoral purposes.'

On Thursday, September 18th, at the North Riding Magistrates Court (held in Scarborough's Court House, Castle Road), Anne Galloway was charged with 'keeping a brothel at Scalby' and Eliza Pearson was charged with 'assisting in the management of the same brothel'.

Appalled by the defendants' immoral careers, the magistrates fined them fifty pound apiece and offered an alternate sentence of 'three months in prison with hard labour'. Both women chose the fine – and each paid £20 on account and agreed to pay the remainder within one month!

Over-drinking and drunkenness were a serious problem once-over too. There was no lack of facilities. Although Scalby had only some 400 or 500 inhabitants, at one time there were three public houses. Before the present inns, familiar to many in Scalby, there were only two recorded in 1823, the Ship Inn, run by Jonathan Hodgson and the Oak Tree, owned by Samuel Stonehouse.[15] Later, in 1840, this same Sam Stonehouse was mentioned as running the Nag's Head Inn,[16] the only public house given for Scalby. However, two unnamed 'beerhouses' were recorded – drinking establishments without a licence to sell spirits. The owners were given as Elliot Dunnill, who between 1855 and 1857[17] was given as the landlord of the Swan Inn, and William Simpson, given as the landlord of the Plough Inn between 1855 and 1857.[18] Interestingly, in 1872 a Mrs Simpson was recorded as running the Plough[19] – no doubt William's widow. Possibly the two beerhouses later applied for full licences and became the two inns respectively?

The Nag's Head Inn, built solidly in stone, occupies a commanding position at the crossroads in the centre of the village. From 1855 to 1872[20] the landlord was Richard Pearson. In 1879, however, we have an historical contradiction: Israel Flinton, of the milling family who worked Newby Mill (see page 58), was given as the landlord. Did he come out in favour of another? An advertisement bill dated later that year gives Stephen Roberts as landlord:

SCALBY

October 31, 1879

**FRIENDSHIP INVITES YOU,
REFRESHMENTS ABUNDANT**

Dear Sir,
 *It is with the greatest respect
imaginable that I invite you to my
SPECIAL ENTERTAINMENT or
BANQUET, which will take place
at the NAG'S HEAD INN, SCALBY,
on Friday, 7th November, at 5 p.m.
Please make it convenient.*

**I am,
faithfully yours,
Stephen Roberts**

Later still, in 1890, Frederick Jarvis was landlord, advertising 'visitors and tourist accommodated on reasonable terms'.[21]

The Temperance Hall, now the Wesleyan Church
Hall. It is the third Temperance Hall in Scalby

A few yards away from the Nag's Head Inn was the old Plough Inn, which later became Lynn's confectioner's shop, the Plough Inn of today being built further east. In 1879 Joseph Hill was landlord,[22] but by 1890 it was run by William Duck.[23]

The third inn was the Swan Inn, in South Street, but it disappeared many years ago. It was said that it ran a 24-hour service at one time, the wife attending to customers by day and the husband by night!

A fourth inn, whose whereabouts are unknown to me, was mentioned in an advertisement dated July 1858:

Scalby.– TO BE LET, and entered upon at Michaelmas next, all that New and Commodious INN, called the 'Lancaster Arms', now being erected in the Village of Scalby, distant about two and a half miles from Scarborough, with Stables and other Outbuildings appertaining thereto.

The above offers facilities for a first-rate Hotel business.

Particulars and Terms may be obtained by application to Mr W. Harrison, Albion Hotel, Scarborough; or to

Messrs. DONNER & WOODALL.
Solicitors.

The heavy drinking of those days set up reaction in the form of the Temperance Movement. A Temperance Hall, built near the pinfold in the village centre, was replaced by a better building with a recreation-room, a reading-room and a meeting-hall.

This Temperance Hall was occasionally put to a use for which it was never intended. Its front door had a high, broad step which made a convenient seat, and there on a morning might be seen hard drinkers who were suffering from a bad hangover, sitting with their heads in their hands waiting for six o'clock to strike, when the public house opposite (Nag's Head Inn) would open.

The excesses of those days have long since disappeared. This may have been due to the missionary work of the Temperance Movement, the curtailment of permitted drinking hours, or to prices. Beer was 1d. or 1½d. a glass, spirits 2d. and a whole bottle of whisky 2s. 8d. prior to the First World War. Undoubtedly, it was the cheapness of drink which led many a man astray and to commit foolishness, as a newspaper report of 1933 recounts:

SCALBY'S QUIETUDE DISTURBED. STORY OF FIERCE STRUGGLE. SCARBORO' MEN FINED.

'I rushed among the four of them and separated Berry and Hunter, who were struggling fiercely together, and then concentrated on Davison and Ellis, who by this time were rolling about on the ground, kicking and struggling like two mad things', declared PC Thomas, giving evidence at the North Riding Police Court on Thursday morning, when three men and a woman were alleged to have wilfully obstructed the highway by fighting at Scalby on July 1st.

An unusual photograph showing a 'fight' outside the Plough Hotel, and suggests that the photographer knowing of the events mentioned, 'staged' the episode. About this period, John William Crosier was proprietor. The original 'Plough Inn' was the building in the foreground, mentioned as such on the 1858 Ordnance Survey map. The mock-Tudor edifice which took the same name, replaced it. However, with the increasing popularity of Scalby as a high-class residential and touring area, the name was soon altered to the Plough Hotel

They were John Davison (42) and Ethel Hunter (40), who, represented by Mr J.S. Snowball, pleaded not guilty. The case against them was dismissed, but a fine of £1 each was imposed on the other two, Albert E. Berry (38) and Stanley Ellis (38), stated to be resident in Scarborough.

Inspector Bean said that about 8.40 on Saturday last the four defendants came out of a Scalby inn and Davison and Hunter got into the former's car. The other two came up and AN ARGUMENT COMMENCED. Eventually Davison called on PC Thomas and complained about the conduct of the other two men. When the officer followed Davison out five minutes later he arrived on the scene opposite the Temperance Hall and found all four defendants engaged in fighting and blocking up the road. There were a considerable number of people gathered round. Eventually the officer had to take the three men to the Falsgrave Police Station. Inspector Bean added that there was no allegation that any of them were drunk, although it may have been that some of the disturbance was due to liquor taken by some of them.

PC Thomas said Davison complained to him that the two other male defendants had taken possession of his car.

'When I got to the scene', said witness, 'I found all four of them fighting furiously in the middle of the road which was blocked'.

'It was impossible for any traffic to pass without seriously injuring some of them'.

Continuing, PC Thomas said he rushed in and separated them, and told them to leave the village, but then all gathered round and started shouting their version of the affair. He had to take the men to Falsgrave Police Station.

Mr Snowball suggested that Ellis was the aggressor. Davison, he pointed out, had complained, and was a much smaller man.

Witness replied he could not say who was the aggressor, but so far as he could see, Davison was having by far THE BETTER OF THE ARGUMENT with Ellis. They were all going at it hammer and tongs. Witness admitted he had not to use force to get Davison to drive the car, he just asked him to do so.

Andrew Murdock Clement, resident in Newby, said he followed the four defendants out of a Scalby inn, and saw Ellis and Berry preventing Davison from driving off. An argument ensued. Ellis assumed what witness thought was a threatening attitude to Davison. Hunter was pushed aside, went on the witness, who declared he walked down as he did not wish to see a woman ill-treated. He saw Ellis strike Davison who retaliated. He was going to separate them, but he was told not to interfere as IT WAS 'A ONE-MAN SHOW'. Hunter, he added, only retaliated verbally, although he agreed with Inspector Bean that there was a commotion.

Answering Mr Snowball, Clement said it seemed to him the fight was forced on Davison.

In reply to this, witness said he had not seen Davison attempt to strike him, nor Hunter go behind and scratch him.

When asked if they had anything to say, Ellis and Berry declared they were sorry it happened.

The Chairman (Mr A.H. Robinson), giving the magistrate's decision, said they considered the proceedings were disgraceful in a quiet village like Scalby.[24]

But it was not always the customer who succumbed to temptation:

Business and domestic worries were blamed for his actions by a former licensee of the Nag's Head Inn, Scalby, Bernard Greaves (34), of no fixed address, when he appeared in the North Riding Magistrates Court at Scarborough today charged with embezzling £245/3/11 belonging to his former employers, Messrs. T. Laughton and Sons, Ltd., between 20 and 28 June.

Greaves, who was represented by Mr G. Harburn, pleaded guilty to the offence, and was put on probation for three years. The magistrate said that they thought Greaves had it in him to go straight.

Inspector J.B. Bumby (prosecuting) said that on the morning of 28 June, Greaves left home to visit a dentist in Scarborough to have some teeth extracted. He returned home at about 2pm and, according to his wife, did not appear to be his normal self. He gave the impression that he was under the influence of drink or suffering from the after-effects of the teeth extraction.

Mrs Greaves went upstairs to prepare the meal, and after the meal there was some argument as to who should make some tea. This was the beginning of a rather serious assault on Mrs Greaves, who eventually made the tea and threw a cup of it at her husband. Greaves then lost his temper, said the inspector, and severely beat his wife, certain words were said during the assault. Greaves then left the premises, and his wife, thinking that he had gone out to cool off, did not worry unduly when he did not return at tea-time.

She carried on the business in the evening, and at 9.30 needed some small change. She went upstairs to a bureau where the week's takings were kept and saw that they were missing. She concluded at the time that her husband had taken them into the firm's head office that afternoon.

When Greaves did not return that night or the following day his wife got very worried. She telephoned T. Laughton and Sons and spoke to the assistant manager, Mr Beresford, who went out to the inn that afternoon and checked the contents of the safe and examined the cash book. He found that a total of £249/4/11 had been taken during that week, and that, after expenses a balance of £245/3/11 was due to the firm. Mr Beresford carried out a check which showed that stocks held and supplied to the inn represented a total selling price of £1,233/14/6, and that the value of liquor sold was £948/9/8. The week's takings of £245/3/11 were some £40 less than the stocktaking indicated.

Greaves was seen by Sgt. Rayson at Scalby about a fortnight later and told that there was a warrant out for his arrest for larceny. Asked if he had any of the money in his possession, Greaves said that he had not. He had only 1/4 on him in cash together with three cheques – for £3/9/1, £2/1/2, and £7/11/8 – payable to his firm. These cheques, said Inspector Bumby, were all that had been recovered of the sum.

When cautioned and charged Greaves replied: 'I do admit to this offence, but would prefer to give an explanation later'. Inspector Bumby said that Greaves was away from Scalby for about a fortnight.

It was said that Greaves was appointed licensee in May 1956. He received a wage of £6/18/6 a week and his wife received £2 a week for assisting him. Accommodation, fuel, and lighting were provided free, and any assistance which was required for the running of the inn was chargeable to his employers. Greaves was fully responsible for all transactions and the cash received. He had to record cash taken in a cash book, and the takings were paid into the firm's head office at Scarborough each week, usually on Fridays. Monthly stock checks were made by the firm.

In a statement to the police, Mrs Greaves had said that her husband had had a considerable experience as a barman, but was not experienced so far as the management of a licensed house was concerned. He often had deficiencies in his stock and was worried about them because he did not know how they came about. He worried about a baby she was going to have.

Inspector Bumby told the court that in a statement Greaves said that he was very inexperienced in the clerical side of the business and he suffered shortages in stock. After about six months he was warned about the position by his firm, which sent an overseer to help him. After that everything went well until his wife was taken to hospital. On June 28 he had five teeth taken out and went for a drink to steady his nerves. He was feeling in a very depressed condition that afternoon and after arguing with his wife decided to take the weekly takings into head office. As he crossed the road near the railway station in Scarborough his mind was in such a state that he wanted to escape from it all. He caught a bus to York and went on to Leeds, Manchester, and London, where he lived on the takings. Greaves also stated that he had decided to send a parcel of £140 home to his wife, but that was stolen from him at a hotel.

Mr Harburn told the magistrates that the offence was committed on the spur of the moment when Greaves was taking the cash to head office. His business and domestic troubles had overwhelmed him at the time. His wife was now standing by him and to send him to prison would wreck his home and family.[25]

NOTES

1. White, Gilbert, *Natural History of Selbourne & Naturalists Calendar*, Blackie & Son Ltd., Glasgow.
2. *Hon . . . of Pickering*, ii, 26; iv, 201.
3. VCH.NR(ii) 1923.
4. *Pipe. R.* 11 Hen. II (Pipe R Soc.), 46; 12 Hen. II, 36; 13 Hen. II, 78; &c. *Pipe. R.* 4 Ric. I, m.4d.
5. Together with the mill and millpond at Cloughton (Pat. 7 Jas. I, pt. xxxiii, no. 1).
6. White's *Yorkshire Directory*, 1840.
7. Cole, John, *Historical Sketches of Scalby, Burniston & Cloughton*, 1829.
8. Kelly's *Directory of North & East Riding of Yorkshire*, 1872.
9. Bulmer's *History & Directory of North Yorkshire*, 1890.
10. Scarborough Directory, 1855.
11. VCH.NR(ii) 1923.
12. Kelly's,01872.
13. Bulmer's, 1890.
14. Cole, op. cit.
15. Baines' *Yorkshire Directory*, 1823.

16. White's, 1840.
17. *Scarborough Directory*, 1855; Kelly's *Post Office Directory*, 1857.
18. Ibid.
19. Kelly's, 1872.
20. Ibid.
21. Bulmer's, 1890.
22. Kelly's *Post Office Directory*, 1879.
23. Bulmer's, 1890.
24. *Scarborough Mercury*, 7 July 1933.
25. Ibid., July 1957.

Although the events of the First World War soon overshadowed the earlier Boer War, many residents of Scalby proudly retained their own account of 'BPs' – Lord Baden-Powell's (founder of the Scout movement) – stand at Mafeking

MAFEKING WON BY AN INNINGS AND 219 RUNS.

LORD EDWARD CECIL, "B.-P.'s" CHIEF OF STAFF.

CHAPTER FIVE

'Lest We Forget'

In 1914 the German 'Kaiser' went to war – and thus Britain and Europe were plunged into the bloodiest conflict of its modern history. Everyone was affected, not least Scalby who did its duty by providing 'men-at-arms', both at home and away.

At home, the area centred on Scarborough, which itself fell under bombardment, supported a 'Home Guard' – a platoon of volunteers attached to the North Riding Volunteer Regiment under the command of Platoon Commander J. Hutton. Away, men fought vigorously and died gloriously, and when it was over no fewer than upwards of two hundred men and women had been in action from Scalby alone, their names recorded on the village war shrine.

Unveiled in January 1918, the monument was presented by Capt. and Mrs W.H.L. Wordsworth:

> It is situated in the triangular piece of ground in the centre of the village in which there also stands the Jubilee fountain. A handsome shrine in woodwork, it is appropriately decorated in an ecclesiastical design, and is the work of a Birmingham firm that specialises in this class of production. A sunny calm afternoon, though with a keen frost in the air, favoured the event, and was in sharp contrast with the bad weather that has been experienced on most days of late.
>
> The actual ceremony [on Wednesday] of unveiling was performed by Mrs Wordsworth in the presence of a large number of villagers and others. The company was very representative in character. It included the members of the Scalby Urban District Council and local gentry, the children of the village school, local Volunteers, Boy Scouts, etc. and the proceedings were enlivened by the presence of the National Reserve Band from Scarborough. Band and Volunteers were in their khaki uniforms, lending a military aspect to the scene, the picturesqueness of which was heightened by the presence of the robed clergy and choir boys of the church.

The ceremony was preceded by a formal procession:

> The Volunteers, Boy Scouts, clergy, school children carrying here and there small flags, and representative persons assembled at the corner of Station Lane and headed by the band, marched to the shrine. The proceedings opened with a hymn 'O God our help in ages past.' The Rev. T. Heppell, Wesleyan minister, led the company in prayer, after which Mrs Wordsworth drew from the shrine the Union Jack by which up to this stage it had been covered, the Volunteers presenting arms and the band playing a few bars of the National Anthem.
>
> The Bishop of Hull then dedicated the shrine.

Addressing the company, the Bishop remarked that it must be with mixed feelings that they gathered together for the unveiling of the war shrine. Such an occasion brought thoughts of sorrow to many hearts. Proceeding he touched on the sacrifices that had been made by the men who had gone out from Scalby, and reminded the company of the sacrifices which were being made also by those at home. The amazing thing to him in coming in person in touch with so many who had had to face the burden and sorrow of bereavement was the way in which they had carried their sorrow and gone on with all the work they were doing here for the country at home. If tinged with intense pride; they were proud to claim relationship with these men who had given up all for us and for the standard of truth and justice and of mercy. They had taught us a lesson that there was something worth more than human life, and that was those things which made life worth the living. Without truth and justice and mercy and chivalry, then human life sank down to the lower basis of the animal, not governed by goodwill and living together in love and peace, but rather a life of ravening animals ever on the look out for some advantage for themselves, ever seeking what they could grab by their own power, ever desirous of gaining wealth and power, not that they might do good but that they might serve self.

They did well to record for all time in their midst those who had given up all for their fellows and in that wonderful way had brought themselves more and more closely into the image of Him, the perfect Man, who gave up all for us.

The Bishop went on to express the gratitude they felt to Captain Wordsworth. The shrine would speak to them as they passed it and breathe the true spirit of patriotism.

In conclusion, a plea was made for that unity of spirit which was characterised by the presence there that day side by side of church and chapel. The last lap of any race was always the heaviest. It was then they needed perseverance, and a fixing of the eye on the goal they had set out to reach. We were there now in the last lap of the war, and he urged all to be steadfast to the end.

The Rev. H. Fox, Primitive Methodist minister, also paid tribute to the service and sacrifice of the men who had stood and were to-day standing between us and peril. They would always look upon the shrine with intense gratitude, and he thought they would be determined on their part to make every sacrifice and service possible. The time would come when victory would have been achieved, but then England would not necessarily be saved. It was only as we English people at home supported the work and sacrifice of the men in the field that our island home would be secure. Our greatest securities were in our sanctities, and if we were to be worthy of the service and the sacrifice that were being rendered on our behalf we must ever look at this as to a symbol of something invisible and recognise the only memorial worthy of these great men was the building up of an English life informed and inspired by the great Christian ideas.

After the singing of the hymn, 'For all the saints who from their labours rest' the Vicar of Scalby (the Rev. W.H. Hesmondhalgh) read the closing prayers, and the Bishop of Hull wound up the proceedings by pronouncing the Blessing.

The company dispersed to the strains of the National Anthem.

Some of the names recorded were more than familiar to the Kidd family, indeed they too had a 'hero' serving, their son, Henry F. Kidd, and as a consequence, the fortunes of the conflict were closely followed. It was not by accident that the bishop made an allusion to this in his address when he said, 'they were proud to claim relationship with these men who had given up all' – and among the pages are pasted cuttings relating to a number of friends, whose deeds and deaths were remembered in the local press and so forth.

Foremost among the losses noted was that of Second-Lieut. Lawrence Rowntree, the only son of the late Mr John Wilhelm Rowntree, and Mrs Rowntree, of Low Hall, Scalby. He was half-cousin to Mr Arnold Rowntree, MP. Mrs J.W. Rowntree was the employer of the Kidd family at that time, and 'Milly' Kidd grew up with, and was a lifelong friend of, his sister, Jean Rowntree, and would undoubtedly have known Lawrence, perhaps played with him, although he was no doubt slightly older.

Second-Lieut. Rowntree, who was only twenty-two years of age when he was killed in action on 25 November, was educated at the Downs School, Colwall; Bootham School, York; Haverford College, USA; and King's College, Cambridge, where he was studying medicine when war broke out. Desirous of doing all he could for his country he joined the British Red Cross Society in 1914, and went to France in the autumn of that year, where he assisted in organising and maintaining the Red Cross service in the north of France and in the unoccupied portion of Belgium. After serving in the Haxby Road Hospital at York, he felt that his service was not strenuous enough, so in the early summer of 1916 joined what is now the Tank Corps, and going to France with the tanks took part in the first advance made by these weapons. On being wounded he applied for a commission, and was gazetted to the R.F.A., and in 1917 went to France for the third time, where he fell in the fighting north-east of Ypres. The Officer Commanding, writing of Second Lieutenant L.E. Rowntree, said that 'Since he has joined the battery he has made himself extremely popular and respected with both officers and men, and whether in action or at rest always performed his duties in the most efficient manner'.

Writing to the 'Yorkshire Herald' Sir Alfred Milner says: I would like to pay a tribute to the memory of this very gallant gentleman. I met him first when he was carrying out his duties at Haxby Road hospital. I was very much impressed with his views of the duties of an Englishman in the present grave crisis of our country's history, and I was not surprised when I heard he had enlisted as a private and gone out to take his share of the terrible hardships and dangers at the front. I was so much impressed with his soldierly qualities that on hearing he had been wounded I asked him if I might have the privilege of recommending him for a commission. He told me he was quite ready to carry on as a private, but felt that as an officer he might have a good influence on his men. I therefore applied for a commission which was readily granted. I had several letters from Lieut. Rowntree, and was immensely impressed by the fine spirit of those letters. He set a fine example, and Yorkshire has lost in him a man she could ill spare. He has made the great sacrifice, and has joined that gallant band of heroes whose names will be for ever cherished in the grateful memories of their fellow citizens.

News was received this morning by his father, Mr Edward Carr, Beaconsfield Villa, Scalby, that his son Corpl. Tom Carr, of the North Riding Battery, R.F.A., Scarborough, had been killed last week, and that he had been buried immediately . . .

Corpl. Carr was well known in Scarborough, where he was employed at Mr Dalton's bookshop, Newborough, and also as a night assistant at the Telephone Exchange.

Mr E. Carr . . . has received a letter from the Officer Commanding the North Riding Battery R.F.A., conveying the sad tidings that his son, Corpl. Tom Adamthwaite Carr was killed in action on the 25th May . . . 'The circumstances were briefly these: About 7am the battery opened rapid fire on the enemy's infantry, which were reported to be advancing. A hostile battery opened fire and the third or fourth shell exploded on the right hand gun wheel, seriously wounding Sergt. G.P. Hill (Whitby), and killing instantly your son (who was gun layer), Gunners Clarke, Rowbottom, and Robinson (Scarborough), and Venus (Hull). Your son's services were particularly valuable to the battery, both as an excellent non-commissioned officer and gun layer, but also as my pay clerk, and I miss him very much. He was buried with his comrades . . .

The kindly feeling of attachment which exists between the Scalby schoolmaster (Mr John Tickle), and his old scholars, is expressed in the following extract from a letter of sympathy in the death of Corpl. Tom Carr, R.F.A., killed in action: 'Tom was known to me ever since he was a little fellow two years old. You know how I esteemed him and how intimate and pleasant were the relations between us. His name stands at the head of our roll of honour in school, and there it will remain as long as the school lasts. His death was the death of a hero. He will be remembered with the bravest of the brave.' This extract well expresses the feeling at Scalby in regard to one who was universally esteemed in the district in which he was well known.

KILLED IN ACTION.– 'I should like to add,' says a correspondent, 'something to the memory of Lance-Corpl. Arnold Coultas, who was killed in action on 5th July. The call to arms had scarcely sounded when he felt it his duty to join and fight for old England. His training was spent in different camps in the south – the greater part at Aldershot. He came out a first-class shot, and was chosen as a sniper, going through a special course of training. Many were the interesting letters received by his friends when in camp life – great events when reviewed by the King of Greece and Lord Kitchener, and he wore Kitchener's blue on his first visit from Aldershot, where he spent his twenty-first birthday.

He counted it a great privilege to be present at the memorial service held in the village church when on his recent leave.

He went to France, August 1915, and in one of his letters he wrote: 'I have brought down my first Hun at a distance of 400 yards, which, of course, was due to my fine rifle and telescope.' He had further instructions while in France behind the firing lines, and was a true marksman. When on his recent visit he took down a gun belonging to his great grandfather and said to his uncle, 'I must keep up my practice when I come home.'

The news of how he fell was received by his friends. From his great chum, Corpl. Overin, who said that as soon as the order was given to attack Jack (that being the name given to him while at Messrs. Wright, Scarborough, where he was apprenticed, and for whom he had great respect), was one of the first to attempt to cross the parapet, but before he was over, a machine gun from the enemy was opened upon them, and he was hit, and never spoke again. Two of his friends laid him at the bottom of the trench. After that the machine gun was put out of action, and 800 yards was added to the British gain, and many prisoners were taken.

Official news was received by his mother on July 15th. He fell on the 5th July, and on the road to the advance passed his younger brother Ronald, in an ambulance, suffering from shell-shock, having been blown several yards, escaping with only a few cuts and bruises and torn khaki. The brothers had a chat together, as they had not seen each other since last October, but the 9th York and Lancaster was joined to another division after being there about two weeks.

The fallen hero (for we feel they are such) wrote on his first khaki photo 'Death before dishonour.' We thank God for all the brave boys who are giving their lives for us, and our hearts beat with pride when we think of them.

The Vicar had his favourite hymn sung on Sunday night: 'Hark, Hark My Soul,' and many tears were shed as the people thought of the young life who four weeks that night had left the village to return to France, where many other village boys are willing if necessary, to pay the great sacrifice – and through the great breaks these words come to us:–

> We who have loved him should rejoice,
> Tho' never more we hear his voice,
> That he has joined the glorious band,
> Who perished for the Motherland.

Official news has been received that Lance-Corporal Wilfred Swalwell, M.G.C., has died from wounds while a prisoner in Germany. Lance-Corporal Swalwell, formerly of Gawne's Cottage, served his time with Messrs W.H. Smith and Co. and went out with the 5th Yorkshire Regiment in the early part of the war. He was taken prisoner on the 27th of May, but did not get into hospital until the 23rd of August, having knocked about from one camp to another in the meantime. He was aged twenty-five and single. The date of his death is given as 10th September, 1918. A brother, Private Harold Swalwell, was killed earlier in the war.

It seems only the other day that Alec McCombie was taking his place for the last time in Scalby Church Choir, and now the news has come that he has found a watery grave in the Mediterranean. His ship was torpedoed on April 15th [1917], but the news came just too late for insertion in the June [Parish] Magazine.

Many of us who saw him on leave last Christmas regarded him then as a soldier 'broke in the wars', and secretly hoped that he would not be called upon for some time to resume active service. But that was not to be. Last September the parish suffered the loss by removal of the family to Uttoxeter but distance in no wise diminishes our sense of deep personal loss in the sacrifice of this young life, neither does it lessen our sympathy with the grief-stricken family.

John Watson, posted missing in 1918, was
subsequently reported 'killed by enemy action'.
He was related to the Kidd family by marriage.
Here he is seen prior to leaving for the 'front'
attired in his uniform as 'gentleman's manservant'
to a resident of Scalby

Finally, in a newspaper cutting headed THE FALLEN BRAVE, news was given of another Scalby hero who was related by marriage to the Kidd family:

Mr John Watson, 13 Dean Street, West Vale, Halifax, and formerly employed under the North-Eastern Railway Company at Whitby, has received official intimation from the War Office that his second son, Lance-Corporal John Watson, 14th Worcestershire Regiment, who was previously reported missing since March 25th 1918, is now presumed to have died on that date or later. The last news received of Lance-Corporal Watson was a letter to his father, from his officer, who, writing in April, last year, said:– 'A sudden advance by the enemy in superior numbers forced us to retire, and it was during the retirement that your son was hit. It was impossible for us to get any of the wounded away, as the enemy were right on top of us.' At the time of his enlistment, Lance-Corporal Watson was in a gentleman's service at Scalby. Three brothers have also served with the Colours:– George, the eldest, with the Tyneside Scottish; William, with the East Yorkshire and Ernest, the youngest, with the Northumberland Fusiliers.

Meanwhile, on the home front, throughout the conflict Scalby carried on. A newspaper cutting recounts how:

The Scalby Women's Service League has taken over the garden lately occupied by Mrs Isherwood, who has granted its use free of charge, and it is being cultivated with the object, we understand, of growing produce for use in hospitals. This is one way the women have found of making themselves useful. Some rough work has to be done to put the garden into good condition, and it was interesting this week to witness the Chairman of the Council, the Master of the Hounds, and one or two other prominent male residents diligently wielding spades and pushing wheelbarrows.

Elsewhere, some families counted the cost in other terms. Details were published of the will of:

Capt. John Lionel Wordsworth, 5th (Royal Irish) Lancers, of Glen Park, Scalby, formerly A.D.C. to the Officer Commanding-in-Chief of the Northern Command, who was killed in action near Ypres on the 4th of November last, aged thirty-two years, [who] left unsettled property to the gross value of £47,711 14s., with net personalty of £35,315 11s 2d.

Probate of his will, dated 23rd November, 1903, with a codicil of the 8th August last, has been granted to his brother, Captain William Henry Laycock Wordsworth of the Glen House, Scalby.

He left £100 to the Scarborough Hospital and Dispensary, £50 to the Cancer Research Fund, and a life annuity of £250 to Edith Allen, as a token of friendship and esteem, and of his appreciativeness of her services, and from her decease an annuity of £50 to her sister, Mary Allen; £100 each to his butler, Austin Edward Joplin, and Mary Cosgrove, formerly servant to his mother; £50 to Emma Webb, wife of his coachman; £500 each to Arthur Harrison Stamford and Percival John Metcalfe, his solicitors and former guardians.

The testor left £250 to Lieutenant Brian Winwood Robinson, of the 5th Lancers, and £100 each to Edwin Winwood Robinson and the Hon. Herbrand G. Alexander, both of the 5th lancers; £50 to Capt. Edgar Hume Sleigh, 5th Lancers; and the residue of his property to his brother, William Henry Laycock Wordsworth. Should his brother leave no issue, he left the ultimate residue of his property as to one-eighth to the wife of his said brother, three-eighths to the said Edith Allen, two-eighths each to Arthur Harrison Stamford, his solicitor and former guardian, and his brother officer, Lieut. Brian Winwood Robinson.

Towards the end of hostilities, when 'home' morale was at its lowest, local newspapers were full of criticism, reprisal and attack on 'bureaucratic' administration and stories of German atrocities; letters flew back and forth in the hope of arousing public sympathy – Col. F. D'Arcy Champney had much to write in 1918 in an effort to raise interest and boost recruitment for the 'last push'.

Sir,– The cry in the street of Scarborough during the war has been, 'Why should mine be taken and not another?' It is said that the town has three shelters. Visitors last August declared our City Fathers were to blame.

May one ask if the Chief Constable, as conducting officer, is to be allowed to take his 400 special constables out to France, where fitting work will be found for each and all? Not one is wanted here, and they would not, like our milkman's son, leave a widow and eight young children.

There is no crime in Scarborough, and, therefore, few policemen are needed. Neither on the occasion of the bombardment was a 'special' wanted to brood over the ruins and look as if he had lost a shilling. Nor is their 'lights out' business a necessity, but a nuisance. If Scarborough was shelled or bombed to bits, it might be awkward for some of us with families and houses but the loss of our lives and belongings would not one bit affect the war. That is the only thing which matters.

Then there is the ambulance shelter – people more like uniformed women than men; not much fight in them, with white faces and gloves, hanging about one refuge near the railway station or another near the GPO. Why cannot they be placed free for combatant service in France, instead of waiting for a stretcher case at home?

Thirdly and lastly comes the Volunteer shelter. There are some gallant old warriors enrolled; but there are others, who do not appear much on parade in public, who want turning out with the specials.

A single-handed business which only concerns the possessor and his belongings is no possible use for ending the war. Large businesses in the West Riding (well known to the writer), such as the King and Queen are visiting this week, admit 'no man is indispensable,' and if anyone at the top or the bottom is wanted, he must go.

Then the women. Take a typical instance: three able-bodied ones to look after a house, and elderly mother, and a non-sporting dog! Or the lodging-house keeper, polishing a door knob or washing a door-step – hardworking, reliable people, who might be earning as much in a few weeks at munitions as they make here in a year, and be all the happier for the change . . .

Scarborough has something better to do than posture as a pleasure resort. Granted some are doing better in and by the war, others are shirking. It is not time for anyone to hang back. Where so many are heroes, it seems invidious to particularise; but the writer's eldest son, after covering the retreat of all his comrades, last to leave, with the enemy thirty yards away, wounded and reported killed, on April 21st was in a fortress on the Danube, and had five light machine-gun bullets in his back, consequently he had to spend most of his time on his back, his legs being paralysed, and had to take morphia to get to sleep. A second son is saving many lives by being prompt to act under shell fire. A third is joining up this summer.

We are as far off the end of the war as ever. Lord Wolseley spoke of the 'Yellow Peril,' but for the Japanese and Chinese . . . to sweep through Asiatic Russia and check the Hun might prove a blessing in disguise. The end is not yet.– Yours truly.

Later, after the shooting was over, came the peace, perhaps best epitomized before the days of the 'Cenotaph' by the dedication of the Tomb of the Unknown Warrior in Westminster Abbey – a national event which reached even into the smaller villages of England such as Scalby, where the Kidd family, moved like so many of the nation, kept as a mark of respect a cutting detailing the event:

After an interval of seven days, during which about a million people passed through Westminster Abbey to pay homage to the Unknown Warrior, the grave of the national hero was filled in. At the very last moment a lady came to the Deanery, bringing with her a maple leaf that had been sent from Canada by a soldier who had earned the Victoria cross at Lucknow. She asked that this should be placed on the coffin before the grave was sealed up, and her wish was carried out. Within half-an-hour the nave had been cleared of people. The Abbey was nearly in darkness, and the Unknown Warrior was at last alone. For three hours the coffin was not touched. An organ recital had been arranged in the Abbey, and it was decided not to close the grave until this had finished. For nearly two hours the organ pealed out, and the Warrior received a fitting last requiem. The recital over, the grave was filled with soil that had been brought for the purpose from the battlefields of France and Flanders. A temporary stone was then placed in position, bearing the following inscription:–

A BRITISH WARRIOR
WHO FELL
IN THE GREAT WAR,
1914–1918.

FOR KING
AND COUNTRY.

GREATER LOVE HATH NO MAN
THAN THIS

With the exception of the last two lines, the inscription is the same as appeared on the shield on the coffin. The permanent stone will be a black marble slab. Just as in the case of the Abbey, the pilgrimage to the Cenotaph was continuously maintained. The deepest reverence was shown by all people passing the monument, and, whether on foot or bus, men bared their heads . . .

The Second World War was less personal than the 'Great War' of 1914–18, and in consequence, fewer cuttings are found pasted into the Kidd journal. It was a much larger, 'political' affair on the whole, and the contents of those few newspaper cuttings retained, reflect this – it was a 'thinking' war. Possibly too, fewer local lads were called up, certainly if they were, not in such numbers as previously. One, however, who was called up, never came back to tell the tale.

A memorial service was held in the Parish Church on Sunday morning in memory of the late Laurence John Hesmondhalgh, son of the Rev. W. and Mrs Hesmondhalgh, The Vicarage, Scalby, who was killed in action in Sicily. The church was full and suitable hymns and anthems were chosen. Austin T. Hesmondhalgh, elder brother of the deceased, read the first lesson. Councillor D. Hesmondhalgh, of Bolton, brother of the Vicar of Scalby, attended, but Miss Lucy Hesmondhalgh, the only other member of the family, resident in England, was unable to do so because of her WRNS duties as Senior Officer at Blundellsands. The Vicar of Scalby, Rev. W. Hesmondhalgh, preached the sermon and in it hinted that he might shortly be retiring [he did so in September 1944]. He said that his son Laurence had been born soon after he and his wife

A scene of devastation in Gladstone Road, Scarborough during the Second World War. 'Milly' Kidd attended school at Gladstone Road, 'cycling in each day from Scalby'

came to Scalby, and his death seemed to herald their departure in the near future. A collection taken amounted to £18/6/8, and together with the £10 left by the deceased, will form the nucleus of a fund for a choir endowment to perpetuate his memory.

The outbreak of the First World War commenced in this area with a naval bombardment of Scarborough; one among a number of east coast towns to be so shelled. The Second World War saw Scarborough under direct attack again, particularly during the years 1940 and 1941.

In the first instance, not a few 'bombs and flares' fell in the surrounding neighbourhood, and a note in the Kidd Journal for 19 August 1940, cryptically states, 'Bomb hit the cottage.' A second wave of bombs, dropped a week later, did slightly more damage than earlier, and merited a short 'censured' paragraph in the local press.

Four or five high-explosive bombs, some of which were of the screaming type, were dropped near a north-east coast town.

A farm house near to which a bomb fell during a previous raid sustained some damage and an elderly man received slight cuts, but there were no other casualties. All the bombs fell either in open country or on the sea shore. The sound of aircraft engines was heard before darkness fell, and enemy planes flew over the district at intervals during most of the night. No anti-aircraft guns were in action. There was considerable searchlight activity.

In the following year, aerial attacks intensified, and much damage was done in and around Scarborough. Bombs fell on houses in Gladstone Street where the school, to which 'Milly' Kidd cycled daily from Scalby, was also hit.

In early March 1941, it was reported that there was much indiscriminate bombing with high-explosives and Scarborough was subjected to an attack by waves of enemy aircraft and a prolonged blitz:

Incendiary bombs were showered in various parts of the town, followed shortly afterwards by completely indiscriminate bombing with high-explosives, some of which were of heavy type. In some incidences bombs were dropped among fire-fighters.

A number of houses were destroyed, and many people were injured.

Fire watchers and A.R.P. workers and civilians dealt successfully with most of the incendiary bombs. Several fell on a hospital, without being allowed to cause damage, and a theatre and dance hall were also struck. Many houses suffered minor damage. A fire occurred at a printing works and a furniture repository was destroyed, but all the fires were quickly put out. Some A.F.S. workers were injured.

Later the attack became less intense, but there was desultory dropping of incendiaries and occasional high-explosive bombs for some hours.

Most of the occupants of a row of seven small houses, which were destroyed by one high-explosive bomb, were trapped among the debris. Two of them were fatally injured and several injured people were rescued. Squads worked throughout the night in an attempt to release three others, a woman and two children. After working for some hours they were able to communicate with the victims, who were uninjured and were able to supply drinks to them.

A considerable number of people were removed from their damaged homes and cared for at rest shelters.

A number of delayed action bombs were dropped during the raid, and some of these exploded later.

Nuns quickly put out one of three incendiary bombs which fell on a convent, and with the help of police and wardens prevented others from causing much damage.

An incendiary bomb which fell through the roof of a theatre soon after the audience had left, lodged in a grille and set the woodwork alight. The stage became involved, but the fire curtain saved the auditorium, and A.F.S. men prevented the fire spreading to the dressing rooms.

A farm foreman and his wife and their two children lost their lives when a farm house in the north-east district received a direct hit during the night. An employee who usually sleeps on the farm, owes his life to the fact that he stayed at a nearby town because of the liveliness of the raid.

The Vicar was first on the scene when an incendiary bomb burst through the roof of a village church. The bomb landed in the main aisle and damaged several pews. The Vicar attacked it with sand and a stirrup pump and kept it under control until fire parties arrived.

Another incendiary went through the roof of the village school and damaged children's desks.

A number of houses in one village were damaged by blast and by incendiary bombs, and in another village a man and his wife who spent the night with friends went home to find the house walls damaged, the ceilings down, and a fire-place blown out by a high-explosive bomb, which had landed in the garden.

A final cutting recalls the spirit which prevailed at the announcement of the end of the 1939–45 war, and is a personal 'Recollection of VE-Day – Odd Memories of a Notable Event of Our Time' (by H.L. Gee, of Scarborough) into which celebrations, I am sure, many of the Scalby residents partook in their own special way:

I thought perhaps in years to come you might like to have a summary of VE-Day to remind you of some of the little things that happened on that great occasion.

Some of us spent hours listening-in [to the radio]. We just couldn't help it. We gathered round the radio as iron filings round a magnet. Winston Churchill's historic announcement, brief, to the point, and final. The King's nine o'clock broadcast, heard throughout the empire – the singing of the National Anthem, which must have stirred millions as they listened. That well-known but rather excited BBC commentator who would keep saying, as he described the cheering crowds round Buckingham Palace:

'And I can see the vast concourse of people stretch down Constitutional Hill,' a slip, of course, for Constitution Hill, rather a different thing, I fancy.

The radio, of course, brought all the empire into one place – the cheers and the rejoicing and the enthusiasm of distant places into the most remote Yorkshire village, so that even in a little spot on the Wolds a few thankful people joined in the shouts of the crowd which greeted the Prime Minister in Whitehall; and, as an old Yorkshireman observed: 'Us from Garton were there wi' all rest on 'em cheering like mad outside Mr Dixon's winder, and 'im wi' his wireless on full blast!'

Flags and bunting spread, rash-like with miraculous speed. You remember how wonderful it was to see people hoisting flags . . . an old gentleman in his shirt-sleeves climbing out of an upper window, and risking his life for king and country; the assistants of a boot and shoe shop forsaking the counter to hang out flags and bunting; the man who let the Union Jack flutter upside down in the breeze till a Boy Scout came along and told him of the evil of his ways; the mother who went marching down one of our main streets, pushing a pram with a little flag and a portrait of the Prime Minister! What a good-humoured crowd it was, held up for several minutes, while somebody strung flags across a busy thoroughfare. Nobody cared. The war in Europe was over . . . and we all had time to spare. 'O.K., chum,' said the taxi-driver to the young man who was responsible for the holdup, 'keep the flag flying, and don't mind me!'

And the favours!

Everybody wore one – one schoolboy I met had seventeen and a grin. The very dogs (you remember) wore red, white and blue ribbons and bows.

A friend of mine who travels in the country a good deal came upon a cow with a Union Jack tied to one horn and the Stars and Stripes to the other.

That's the sort of thing they do in Yorkshire. For myself, I wore a favour for twenty-four victorious hours before somebody pointed out that it wasn't really in honour of the victory but a 'left-over' from the Coronation! But then, I'm that kind of chap.

And the services that day. I hope you remember them – or those of the day after. There was something deeply moving about the congregations of thankful people, humble people who met together to give thanks. They met in the great cathedrals and in the little chapels. They met in the old churches and in the new huts erected here and there for workers. There was one Yorkshire village where six farmers were in the pulpit together, and all six gave thanks; and there was another Yorkshire spot where a repatriated prisoner of war read the lesson and a wounded airman gave the little address that followed.

A friend of mine who hails from Ossett remembers vividly the night of VE-Day and how, hearing the church bells pealing out the gift of peace, he climbed a dusty and winding spiral stair in an old church tower, opened a door, and found the bell-ringers toiling and sweating in a room below the belfry. It was an unforgettable sight – the men who so gladly laboured to fling out the joyous news to every homestead for miles.

I think one of the happiest of all the VE-Day features (whichever day you choose) was the way in which little communities gathered together and gave the children a royal time. I remember how housewives baked when they might have been celebrating victory by 'taking things easy,' how they made a bumper tea for half a hundred children, and how the young folk tucked in with a will. I myself shared in an outdoor tea, sitting down side by side with an urchin who kicked my shins as proof of his gratitude for victory. We were at a table in a street, the traffic going by, a fly in my cup, but a great spirit of merriment among us, and all the bairns thrilled to bits, which was just as it should be. Later I ran a race, but got beaten by a five year old, and thoroughly enjoyed it.

Then, of course, the night came on and the stars came out, and the bonfire craze was rife.

Odd, that after so much blackout, illuminated only by fires from incendiaries, we should celebrate by building bonfires and letting off squibs [fireworks], but we did.

We burned old Hilter well and truly. We made a crooked Nazi Swastika, and burned that. It did us good, somehow. It seemed to spell *finis* to the war in Europe. We joined hands (boys and girls and older folk who ought to have had more sense) and danced round the flickering flames, and sang Auld Lang Syne and God Save the King, and then went home to listen-in till one in the morning, for nobody wanted to go to bed . . . you don't get a day like that often in a lifetime.

THE PITY OF IT

She bravely bears
The woman's part,
And shows the world
A hopeful heart,
And turns to all
A smiling face –
Of craven doubt
There's not a trace.

Alone at night
Within the room
Which once they shared,
Forebodings loom;
If he should ne'er
Come back – what then?
If he should fall
Like other men!

The mask drops off
The smiling face;
The bosom heaves
Beneath its lace;
She kneels beside
The empty chair –
The loneliness
Is hard to bear!

'I want him, God –
I want him so!
If he should die –
Not that, God no!
Blind, crippled, dumb,
Or helpless, Jack,
What matters that
If you come back?'

'I'll slave for you
Till fingers bleed,
That you may rest
And never heed;
You shall not lack

A single thing;
My life for you –
My Heart, my King!'

The dying coals
Fall in the grate,
The room grows cold,
The hour is late;
In weariness
She droops her head;
She sleeps, and dreams
He is not dead!

Yet out in France,
'Neath starlit skies,
Her loved one's well
Remembered eyes
Look up above,
Yet do not see –
Ah, God that things
Like War should be!

R.A.H. Goodyear

NAMES ON THE WAR MEMORIAL

The shrine bears the following list of names, those marked with a star having been killed
in action or died of wounds:

Oliver Parkin Abram
Jack Appleby
Tom Appleby
Thos. W. Armstrong
Edward Atkinson
Joseph K. Atkinson
Herbert Barker
Geo. H. Bastiman
George Bird, VC*
Norman Bird
Austin Boddy
Bernice Boddy
James Alf Boddy
Walter Boddy
Wilfred Boddy
C. Bowes
George Bowman*

David Boyes
G. Boyes
Frank Bray*
Charles Broughton
John Brown
Wm. J. Brown
Frank Carr
Tom A. Carr*
Herbert Chadwick
Gilbert Cockerill
William Collinson
Albert Cook
Arthur Cook
Sydney Cook
Colin Coulson, DCM
G.H. Cook
J. Cook

David R. Coulson
Alfred Coultas
Arnold Coultas*
C. Ronald Coultas
Reginald M. Coultas*
Horace Cox
Walter Cox
Barnard Dobson
John Douglas
Henry Douglas
James Drummond
Ernest Dugdale
John Robt. Dugdale
Wm. Dugdale
Frank A. Dunkley*
Alexander T. Dunkley
Albert C. Dunkley
Frank Dunn
Fred Dunn
George Emmerson
Valentine Emmerson
A.H. Fawcett
G.H. Fawcett
R. Fearnside
Albert Fletcher
Leslie D. Fletcher
Frank J. Flinton
Israel Flinton
L.J. Fox
William Forster*
Geo. H. Goodwill
Jno. Wm. Goodwill
Frank Hardwick
R. Harper
Harry Heath
Alfred Hill
G.L. Wick*
Albert Horsley*
H. Humpleby
Francis R. Hurd
Fred Hurd
George Hurd
Robinson Hurd
E. Ingham
O. Ingham
James Albert Iveson

Stanley F. Jarvis
Wm. Jarvis
Wm. Jennings
Charles Johnson
Elspeth Johnson
J.Wm. Johnson
George Johnson
William C. Johnson
Harold Jones
Henry F. Kidd
A. Leadill
Wm. Leadill
S.S. Lockwood
Willie Lord
A.G. Lotinga
Chris. Leadley
Fred Lummas
George Lyon
W. Lyon
George Mann
H.J.E. Marsden
Harry Mitchell*
C. Mitchell
W. Mitchell
John Wilson Morley
F. Moody*
Basil Moxon
H.R. Moxon
Alec McCombie*
Wm. McCombie
William Newman
Thos. Nellist
Wm. Nellist
Walter Newham*
J.H. Nicholson, MM
M.G. Norris
Edward C. Peacock
Tom Pickering
Frank Power
E.W. Putman
W.E. Putnam
Louis Raine
Ernest Raney
Stanley Raney
Wm. Ralph
Harold Raw

N. Reid

Wm. O. Readman

Lawrence Rowntree*

Ernest H. Rudgard

Alfred Hugh Rudgard

C.K. Ruddock

John Sedman

Ernest H. Sellers

Fred Sellers

James Sharp

Wm. Shaw

James Shearsmith

Tom Shearsmith

Bryan Shepherd

Edward Shepherd

George Shepherd

Herbert Shepherd

John Shepherd

William Shepherd

Dickenson Simpson

Charles Sillery*

Harry Smith

Claude Robinson

George Robinson

Thos. Robinson

John Steel, sen.

J. Steel, jun

Thos. P. Steel

Wm. Steel

Geo. Stonehouse

Richard Stonehouse

Harry Taylor

T. Taylor

D. Tenison

Fred Thompson

Oliver Thompson

Eric Tickle

Gordon Tickle.

John D. Tickle

Leslie Tickle

Fred Tipping

Robt. A. Smith

Chris. Southwick

Frank Sparkes

Wm. Tipping

James Todd*

Charles Toft

Harry Toft

Geo. Trattles

Wm. Trattles

Geo. W. Turner

Eric Tyson

E.M. Varley

Cesar Veighe

Robt. H. Ward

Wm. Ward

John Watson

Arthur Webb

Wm. White

Frank Whittaker

Lionel Wilsher

R.H.S. Wilkinson*

Lionel J. Wordsworth*

W.H.L. Wordsworth

Frank A. Wrightson*

James Yeoman

Frank Yewdall

CHAPTER SIX

Family Affairs

The Kidd family came to Scalby in 1883. They came, Henry and Hannah, with three children, to their employer's newly built house – The Holt. Henry had been coachman with Mr J.A. Cooke for over fifteen years by then. They had come from Hull, at least that is where their youngest child, Edwin, had been born about the time Henry had come into service with Mr Cooke. Indeed, at the age Edwin came to Scalby, he was old enough to take a position himself, as coachman with Mr Cooke, working alongside his father – a satisfactory arrangement all round, and one which undoubtedly showed the regard with which Mr Cooke held Henry Kidd, for Edwin's elder brother, Charles Thomas, was also recently in the employ of Mr Cooke, on the staff of his newspaper, *The Hull Daily News*. Their middle child and only daughter, Frances Hannah, it appears, stayed at home and helped mother run the house, which at

A typical brewery yard in the nineteenth century as might be known to Hannah Kidd, whose father, John Warley, was a brewer in Bridlington at this period

Bridlington Priory. It was here, in gardens behind the priory, that 'Milly' Kidd's great-grandfather dug up a coin dated 1566

that time, was Holt Cottage, set aside by Mr Cooke for the use of the coachman's family.

Their mother, Hannah, was a native of Bridlington, the youngest of twelve children. She was born in 1837, the year Queen Victoria came to the throne. Her father, John Warley, was a brewer in the town. Little is recorded of him except a short, handwritten note penned after his death stating how 'a Queen Elizabeth shilling was dug up in a garden at Bridlington dated 1566 in the year 1866 by John Warley, brewer, of Bridlington, just 300 years old, and now in the possession of his daughter Hannah Kidd in Scalby 1921. The Queen's effigy was very clear.' A number of years later in February 1937, this was reprinted with additions in the local press:

> A discussion on old coins has been taking place in our columns recently, and Mr Edwin Kidd, of 2 Curraghmore Terrace, Scalby, informs us that he has in his possession a shilling of the reign of Queen Elizabeth, dated 1566. This was dug up by his grandfather while working in his garden at the back of the old Priory Church, Bridlington, over 100 years ago. It is in a good state of preservation.

John Warley had at least one brother Henry, and one sister. She married Capt. William Scott, of Hull, and an offspring of their union, the eldest, William Henry, cousin to Hannah, was drowned on 16 February 1879, when the SS *Jura*, of Glasgow, sank on the Yarmouth Cross Sands. At the time the steamship met its untimely end on a regular voyage between Hull and Cyprus and Smyrna, William Henry was first mate, aged thirty-five, of Russell Street, Hull.

A newspaper cutting, one of three accounts, pasted in the family album, recalls in detail the supposed fate of the SS *Jura* and its crew of eighteen (mainly Greeks):

The following is the report of William Snook, water-clerk of Messrs. Turrill and Torkildsen, of Great Yarmouth: – Deponent was called up at 4am on February 17th, in consequence of signals having been seen on the Cross Sand, and finding the steamtug Pilot going out, went on board and proceeded from Yarmouth at 5am. At 6.30am, tide being half flood, weather hazy, wind N.E. blowing light with a heavy swell of sea from the N.E., the steamtug having previously spoken to the St Nicholas Lightship, the master of which stated that he had seen no signal of distress, proceeded to the eastward of Cross Sand, and cruised about till daylight, when at 7.30am they fell in with a quantity of wreckage, apparently of a steamer, there being the greater part of her poop (half round), hatches, and other portions of the deck of a steamer. The tug steamed amongst the wreckage, and they saw two boats, and took one in tow which was full of water, and left the other, which was too much damaged. The boat was marked, 'S.S. Jura, Glasgow'. They also picked up a medicine chest marked the same.

Deponent observed what he supposed was the head of a body floating, but before the tug could be stopped it disappeared. An engineer's logbook was also picked up belonging to the Jura. The articles mentioned were, on arrival of the steamtug in Yarmouth harbour, delivered to the Receiver of Wrecks. The Jura is supposed to be totally lost with all hands. Nothing more has yet been heard of the ill-fated steamer, nor of any of the crew, and it is not doubted that all have perished. The deck of the steamer has been found completely separated from the other part of the vessel, and this with other evidence, points to an explosion on board as the most probable cause of the wreck. This is now generally believed to be the most reasonable solution of the mystery. The keeper of the St Nicholas Lightship reports that he has seen no sign of distress from the direction of the Cross Sand; and, as there was almost an entire absence of wind on the night of the disaster, it seems highly improbable that the steamer would have grounded with sufficient force to break up in so short a time.

Henry Warley, John's only brother we know about, lived at Pasture House, Beeford, in the East Riding. He had a number of children, and two daughters it is recorded, married: Sarah Ann, second daughter, on 5 February 1891, at the Priory Church, Bridlington, by the Revd Dr Given, to Joseph Sugden, of Huddersfield; and Mary, third daughter, on 23 September the year previous, at the village church of St Paul's, Beeford, by the Revd L.W. Higgins, vicar of Foston, to John Alfred Wilcox, of Scarborough.

Henry Kidd was born at Ellerker, a small village in the East Riding (now Humberside). From what size family he came, we are not told, but it would appear he had at least a sister, as a nephew of the same name as his father, was somewhat of a poet, and on the death of his father's employer, he had published a eulogy entitled 'LINES COMPOSED BY ISAAC SWINTON, Jun. *Addressed to his father, Gardener at Manby Hall,* On the death of his late Master, W.T. Welfitt, Esq. WHO DIED ON THE 25th OF JANUARY, 1864'.

It would appear Henry's own early employment was at Ellerker Hall as coachman, as there exists an altered and dated engraving of a coach and horses depicted on its journey

Nephew of Henry Kidd, Scalby

LINES COMPOSED BY ISAAC SWINTON, Jun.,

Addressed to his Father, Gardener at Manby Hall,

On the death of his late Master, Wm. T. Welfitt, Esq.,

WHO DIED ON THE 25TH OF JANUARY, 1804.

He has gone to the grave, a companion of many,
  And has left us a brilliant example behind;
So mild was he always, and gentle as any,
  And was he not always so thoughtful and kind.

You'll miss him at morn, when in view of the study
  You look for a smile with a pleasing good morn;
And feel, as you look on that corner so woody,
  The loss of a master that did it adorn.

You'll miss him at noon when the sun shines in splendour,
  And the dew from the earth has vanished away;
His voice you'll not hear grateful praises to render,
  Or thankfully speak what a beautiful day.

You'll miss him when summer is here in its beauty,
  When the rose and carnation appear in full bloom;
You'll gather no more as a part of your duty
  To decorate one who now lies in the tomb.

You'll miss him when little improvements you're making,
  Or when you've been cleaning and making all neat;
How would he approve when pains you'd been taking,
  And ever and anon would praises repeat.

You'll miss him when viewing his noble supporter,
  I speak of his mare so faithful and true;
And think of the days when he frequently rode her,
  His calling of justice to go and pursue.

You'll miss him when bells from the tower are calling
  The villagers all to assemble at kirk;
'Twill renew in your mind the fact so appalling,
  He has gone to the grave,—he has finished his work.

You'll miss him when trimming the grave where he's sleeping,
  When flowers appear on his turf covered bed;
And know that above his reward he is reaping,
  While his body now lies with the slumbering dead.

The published poem of Isaac Swinton, Junior, who was a nephew of Henry Kidd of Scalby

A steel engraving showing 'Coach and Horses' that has seen alteration and dated in Henry Kidd's handwriting, who was a coachman at Ellerker Hall, in the East Riding (now Humberside)

from the Hall. On leaving there, the family still took an interest, and an advertisement published on the sale of Ellerker Hall reveals the extent and nature of the estate as they knew it:

ELLERKER HALL ESTATE, EAST YORKSHIRE
TO BE SOLD BY AUCTION,
BY MR. W.N. LEWENDON.

At the ROYAL STATION HOTEL, Hull, on TUESDAY, August 30th, at Half-past Two for Three o'Clock in the afternoon, subject to such conditions as shall be then read, and which may be seen on application to the Auctioneer, or to the undermentioned Solicitors, three days prior to the day of sale.

ALL that capital Freehold country RESIDENCE, known by the name of 'Ellerker Hall' situated at Ellerker in the East Riding of the County of York, containing Entrance-Hall, three Reception-rooms, four principal and other Bed-rooms, newly fitted Bath and lavatory with hot and cold water, good Kitchens, Butler's Pantry and other conveniences, together with Stabling for six horses, good Harness-rooms, newly erected Coach-house which will hold four carriages, Wash-house, Cow-house, Piggery, hen-house, excellent Kitchen Garden well stocked with fruit trees, tastefully laid out Ornamental Pleasure Garden with Croquet Lawn, two Green-houses and Vinery, and the newly-erected Gothic Lodge.

Also all those four grass PADDOCKS, two of which are situate in front of the Hall (enclosed with iron fence), and two at the back, having extensive frontages to the highroads.

Also all that COTTAGE and plot of Freehold LAND, containing 23 perches or thereabouts, situate in the village of Ellerker aforesaid, now in the occupation of Mr Thomas Sparks, which cottage is now used as a post-office.

And also those Two COTTAGES or TENEMENTS and Garden, situate in the village of Ellerker, now in the occupations of Messrs Tidbrook and Rogers. These last-mentioned premises are copyhold of the Manor of Howden.

The whole of the above Estate is now held by Henry Smith, Esq., and his undertenants, at the very low rental of £110 per annum, and comprises an area of 11 acres or thereabouts.

The Residence is approached by a half-circle carriage drive with double entrance gates.

There is an excellent supply of pure water. It is thickly and very ornamentally timbered and surrounded by a beautiful and well-wooded country, not far distant from the River Humber, and is worthy the attention of any one seeking a desirable country residence.

Any purchaser not requiring the whole of the land and cottages might let part off for about £40 per annum, without detriment to the residence and pleasure grounds.

Ellerker Hall is within 15 minutes drive of the Brough Station, on the North-Eastern Railway, and is about 1½ miles from Cave and the new station of the Hull and Barnsley Railway.

An embossed invitation card from a servants(?) function at Burton Constable Hall (EY) showing, on the reverse, a list of dances performed

Theatre Royal,

BURTON CONSTABLE.

MARCH 28th, 1856.

THIS EVENING WILL BE PERFORMED

THE FARCE OF

"HIGH LIFE BELOW STAIRS!"

Lovel (a Young West Indian of Fortune) .... MR. JAY

Freeman (his Friend)............ HON. T. E. STONOR

Philip, ⎫
Tom, ⎬ Servants to Lovel .... ⎧ MR. MANSFIELD
Kitty, ⎭   ⎨ MR. E. LANE
                                                                             ⎩ MISS CHICHESTER

Duke's Servant, ⎫   ⎧ MR. LEE
Sir Harry's Servant, ⎬ Visitors........   ⎨ MR. C. SEARLE
Lady Bab's Maid, ⎬   ⎨ MISS PALMER
Lady Charlotte's Maid ⎭   ⎩ LADY CLIFFORD CONSTABLE

Stage Manager .... HON. T. E. STONOR.

Vivat Regina.

One of two handbills produced in 'fun' for productions staged for the benefit of the servants and staff, and performed by family and friends of the Chichester-Constable's, of Burton Constable Hall (EY)

Later, Henry held a position at Burton Constable Hall, seat of the Chichester-Constable family. Indeed, it is probable that it was here Henry and Hannah met, his wife-to-be possibly in service too, coming from nearby Bridlington.

There is no record of when they married, but it would be around this time, and a number of items dated in the late 1850s confirm their employment at Burton Constable Hall; an extensive account of the twenty-first birthday celebrations of Mr (Lieut.) Raleigh Chichester-Constable records that apart from the main celebrations for three hundred invited distinguished guests from 'all parts of the county . . . The tenants on the East Riding estate and tradesmen were similarly entertained last evening, and for Boxing Day the servants and staff have been invited to a ball'.

An embossed invitation card bearing the family arms and title 'Burton Constable', dated 23 February 1857, gives a list of dances to another festive occasion. Elsewhere, other celebratory events are recorded in the form of two printed handbills displaying separate theatrical productions at the 'Theatre Royal, Burton Constable' on the evenings of 27 and 28 March 1856, when the servants and staff were entertained by the family and friends playing the roles of 'servants' in two farces – *Unfinished Gentleman* and *High Life below Stairs*. Indeed, it would seem that despite the hard work expected, for those in service there was never a dull moment and much 'high life below stairs'.

The eldest son of Henry and Hannah, Charles Thomas, married, and the couple lived in Scalby; in 1902, however, they left the village for Hull. Friends and colleagues of Mrs C.T. Kidd held her in high esteem and a presentation was arranged prior to her departure:

An interesting gathering of the Scalby branch of the Mothers' Union was held in the Temperance Hall, Scalby on Thursday evening. This branch of the society, under the able management of Miss Barker, the Hon. secretary, has for some years past done excellent work in providing and making garments for Dr Barnardo's Home, and one of its most energetic members is Mrs Kidd, who has been a well-known and much-respected resident of the village for nearly twenty years. Mrs Kidd is now leaving Scalby to take up her residence in Hull, and members and associates of the Mothers' Union testified the esteem and regard in which she has been so deservedly held by them by presenting her with a very handsome solid silver sugar basin, of Queen Anne pattern, bearing the inscription, 'Presented to Mrs Kidd by the members of the Scalby branch of the Mothers' Union, 1902'. The presentation was made on behalf of the subscribers by the vicar of Scalby (the Rev. W. Cautley Robinson), who felt in a few well-chosen words expressed the general regret which is felt at the departure from Scalby of Mrs Kidd, who has always been an active worker in every parochial movement. Mrs Kidd having responded, the meeting terminated.

Sadly, their move to Hull was short-lived. On 26 June the following year Charles Thomas died, and from the printed obituary it appears his wife, by this time, had also passed away, as no account mentions a 'bereaved widow' left to grieve, nor it seems, was there any issue. Aged forty-two he

died very suddenly. . . . Mr Kidd was on holiday at Cloughton where his brother resides, and up to within an hour of his death, which was due to sudden heart failure, he was in his usual health and cheerful spirits. . . . [He] was for many years

Edwin W. Kidd in 1886, shortly after arriving at Scalby

Edwin W. Kidd in 1926, possibly seated in his own front room?

associated with the staff of the *Hull News*, having entered the office as a lad. He was the son of the late Mr Henry Kidd, of Scalby, formerly of Ellerker, and for many years in the employ of Mr J.A. Cooke, the proprietor of the *Hull News*. Mr Kidd the younger, continued with the latter as clerk and bookkeeper up to the time of the amalgamation in 1898 of the *Hull News* with the present company, to whom his services were transferred, and with whom he remained up to the time of his death.

Some time ago he was laid aside for several months with a severe illness, and returned to business about 18 months ago. He was last week away on a holiday with his brother, who resides at Cloughton [Cober Hill], when on Friday night he was taken ill and passed away within the hour.

Mr Kidd was of a quiet unobtrusive nature and kindly disposition. He was most trustworthy, and possessed the confidence and esteem of his employers, by whom as well as by all his colleagues he was highly respected. His sudden and unexpected death is greatly deplored.

The funeral took place on Monday in the picturesque churchyard of Scalby, near Scarborough. The chief mourners were, the deceased's mother, brother, and sister, and there were also present Mr A. Tidman (representing Mr J. O'Hara, the editor-manager of the *Eastern Morning* and *Hull News* Company) and Mr W. Stalker

Henry Francis Kidd (1898–1986), grandson of Henry Kidd, of Scalby and formerly of Ellerker. His father was Edwin Warley Kidd

Louisa Ellen Kidd, wife of Edwin Warley Kidd, mother of Henry Francis and Florence Mildred 'Milly' Kidd. It was her mother, Hannah, who started the family album in the 1880s

(cashier), who placed on the coffin a wreath sent by the deceased's fellow-employers. There were several other floral devices, including one from Mrs J.A. Cooke.

The service was impressively conducted by the Rev. W.C. Robinson (vicar of Scalby), assisted by the Rev J.T. Tause (vicar of Cloughton), the former in the church paying a high tribute to the personal qualities of Mr Kidd.

Frances Hannah, the beloved and only daughter of the late Henry Kidd and Mrs Kidd, of 4 Jubilee Terrace, Scalby, passed away 27 January 1915. She remained unmarried and died aged forty-nine.

Their youngest son, Edwin Warley Kidd, was the only one to survive, marry and produce grandchildren. Born in 1867, he died after a short illness in 1941 aged seventy-four. He was held in high regard by the village.

Edwin's address at his date of death was given as 2 Curraghmore Terrace, Scalby, which he possibly took at the time of his retirement in 1925 when leaving his employment at Low Hall. He was a native of Hull, coming to Scalby at the age of sixteen or thereabouts. His first period of employment was in the service of Mr J.A. Cooke, of Scalby Holt, as coachman, working at first alongside his father, Henry. It was during this time, that Edwin and Lousia Kidd's first child, Henry Francis was born 13 March 1898. It

Curraghmore Terrace, Scalby. It was at No. 2 that the Kidd family lived for many years

Edwin Kidd at work. He was employed, prior to his retirement in 1925, by the Rowntree family. He is seen here with the grandchildren of Mrs J.W. Rowntree

is not known, however, when Edwin married his wife, nor the circumstances of their meeting. Not long afterwards, Edwin moved his employment and family to Lord Airedale, at Cober Hill, Cloughton. It was while working here, that his brother Charles died on a visit in 1903 – two years after the birth of Edwin's second child, a daughter, baptized Florence Mildred 'Milly' in St Laurence's Church, November 1901.

Nine years later, Edwin returned to nearby Scalby, and took up his final employment, in service with the widow of Mr John W. Rowntree, the cocoa and chocolate manufacturer of York and social reformer. Mrs J.W. Rowntree lived at Low Hall. The obituary of Edwin Kidd states that he was for many years a sidesman at Scalby church.

Edwin's father, Henry Kidd, died in 1896, never seeing his grandchildren. His short obituary reveals a little of the man who died while still in service with Mr Cooke:

> It is not often that a village funeral attracts so large an attendance of sympathetic friends and spectators as was witnessed on Tuesday at the internment of Henry Kidd, for twenty-four years the valued servant and coachman of Mr J.A. Cooke. The service was conducted, in the absence of the Vicar, by the Rev. T.W.T. Hart, MA, Rector of St Cuthbert's, Hawick, Scotland. At the conclusion of the portion of service read in the church, Mr Hart gave a brief address, in which he said that the chief object in life was to discover and lead the true religious life, the Christianity which Christ taught. What was that life? It consisted of two things, and neither was complete without the other: Devotion to God; duty towards man. That, and that alone, comprehended the entirety of religion. This great object of life their brother whose remains they were now committing to peaceful rest had sought for, and attained in large measure. For nearly a quarter of a century, respected and esteemed by all who knew him, Henry Kidd had been a valued servant to his employer. In these days of constant, restless, ever changing service, that was a noteworthy fact. Such a period tended inevitably to gradually efface the ordinary distinction of master and servant, to raise the latter into the position of a valued and trustworthy friend, whose advice on matters within his own special experience was esteemed. Their departed brother was a man whose religion was as earnest as it was retiring. He loved his Church, and, when ill-health forbade his attendance there, always followed the appointed service for the day in his Prayer Book. It was surely with something more than hope that they would now lay him in the quiet precincts of that hallowed ground.

> On Sunday last, the Rev. Mr Rickes, of Harrogate, after speaking of Christ's fellowship with men in their trials, temptations, and sufferings, said, 'I am reminded at this moment of the shadow of bereavement which has fallen upon this parish, and upon this church, in the death of one of its members, and I ask you to carry to the bereaved family the sweet message of the Gospel that comes to your own hearts this morning. Will you go and tell those sorrowing ones of the love of Him who was the Man of Sorrows, and who wept with them that wept? Will you tell them not to sorrow as men without hope; for through the sufferings, death, and resurrection of Christ, beyond the shadows, and beyond the tomb they shall meet that husband and that father again, and stand with him in the light and bliss of heaven, in the perfect peace of the home of the sons of God'.

Edwin and Louisa Kidd (left) taken Whit Monday, 1927

Somewhat poignantly, handwritten notes dated Sunday 12 April 1868, made at the time of the Revd Rickes' sermon, given at Scalby in the absence of his widow and children, are preserved in the Kidd family album, retained as a memorial to the departed Henry Kidd.

Henry's widow, Hannah Kidd, went on to outlive her husband by thirty years. On his death, she took up residence at 4 Jubilee Terrace, living with her daughter, Frances, until the latter's death in 1915, then alone until 1926 when Hannah herself died, aged eighty-nine, well remembered and respected in the village and 'one of Scalby's oldest residents'. On her death it was recorded that 'since just before Christmas Mrs H. Kidd . . . had been in ill-health, and on the Monday afternoon she passed away at the above address'. At the time of her passing, Hannah still had a sister (one of twelve) residing at Bridlington, aged ninety-four. 'Mrs Kidd took a great deal of interest in the village church life, and in earlier years was a regular attender at the services.'

A year later, a current issue of the 'Parish magazine' [contained] the following tribute to the late Hannah Kidd. 'Life's race well run' may be truly said at the passing of Hannah Kidd. Full of years – she would have been 90 on February 6th – held in high esteem by friends and acquaintances, a good and zealous churchwoman, with unflagging zeal in good works, she has entered into the rest of Paradise, where her works have followed her. It is given to few in her station of life to enjoy and employ so fully the faculties of mind and body. A real 'Mother in Israel'. A pattern indeed for latter-day mothers to emulate, if they would command the love and duty of their children.

'Grannie' Abram, of Burniston, in all her maternal glory

Never remarrying, Hannah Kidd, herself coming from a large family, was related through marriage, into an even larger one – the Abram family – one of distinction in the neighbourhood, and through this connection, was a member of an enormous 'extended' family which reached all parts of Yorkshire and beyond:

The funeral of the late Mrs Abram took place on Saturday [29 December 1923: died 26 Dec]. A service was held in the Wesleyan Chapel at 2.30 pm, conducted by Mr T. Barrett and Rev. W. Hesmondhalgh, Vicar of Scalby. There was a large gathering of relatives and friends an evidence of the love and respect for Mrs Abram by all who knew her. Out of her fifteen sons and daughters, it is believed that thirteen were present at the funeral. The hymns, 'Jesu, Lover of my Soul' and 'Rock of Ages' were sung during the service. There were many beautiful floral tributes of love. On Sunday evening a special memorial service was held in the Wesleyan Chapel in memory of the late Mrs Abram, conducted by Mr R. Frankish. Mrs Abram was the oldest member of the church, having reached the age of 83. She became a member of Mr Severs' class when she first came to live at Scalby and has taken a delight in attending the services when she was able. There was a good attendance of friends and relatives at the service and Mr Frankish, taking as his text, 'So he bringeth them unto their desired haven', spoke of his personal knowledge of Mrs Abrams, of her long and useful life, her unfailing cheeriness, and her beautiful old age. Appropriate hymns were sung and at the close the choir gave 'For all the Saints'.

She and her husband, Francis Abram (b. 1823), son of a well-established family in Burniston, formerly carried on a dairy farming business at Cockrah Farm, and afterwards, removed to Clarence House, Burniston. Mr Abram's father, John Abram, and his wife, lived at one time in the house once occupied by Mr W. Lee, and in a full and rewarding life, were witnesses at the trial which followed the dramatic shooting tragedy at Burniston in February, 1823 (see page 38). They, removing to Burniston from Scalby, where John Abram and his wife lived for a period at Yew Court, before financial constraints forced them to move.

At the time of Mr and Mrs Francis Abram's Golden wedding in 1908, they had 15 children – twelve daughters and three sons – all of whom survived and married, except two, and there was a total of 40 grandchildren! Three of the daughters resided at Scarborough, one being Mrs Crawford, wife of the caretaker of Gladstone Road Schools, and another the wife of the coachman of Mr Kirk, brewer. One daughter, the wife of Mr Tindall, blacksmith, lived at Harwood Dale, two resided at Burniston, one at Bishop Auckland, one at Harrogate, one at Sutton, and one lived at Terrington. Two sons and a daughter resided near Leeds.

Edwin and Louisa Kidd, taken at Scalby in 1941, shortly before Edwin died

Florence Mildred 'Milly' Kidd (1901–79), daughter of Edwin and Louisa Kidd

Silver Wedding of Henry F. Kidd (29 September 1954) with his sister, 'Milly' (left) and his wife Madge (née Marguerite Thornton)

Francis Abram married his bride Ann at Scalby parish church on December 18th, 1858, even though he was born and lived his whole life in Burniston. The ceremony was conducted by the Rev. Sedgwick. At the time of their Golden Wedding 50 years on, when Mrs Abram was 68 and her husband 75, it was said that Mrs Abram regularly walked into Scarborough each market day. The occasion of their Golden wedding was honoured by the presentation of a purse of gold by their children.

Meanwhile, Henry Francis and Florence Mildred, the children of Edwin and Lousia Kidd, were growing up in Scalby. Henry was born at Holt Cottage while his father worked for Mr James A. Cooke. At the outbreak of the 1914–18 hostilities, he was of an age to be 'called up' and was, serving in France.

It is not known what became of Henry F. on his return from the war, the only newspaper cutting is an account of his wedding at St Mary's parish church, Scarborough, undated, which recalls his marriage to Marguerite (Madge), daughter of Mr & Mrs A. Thornton, of 45 Newborough, Scarborough:

The Rev. Watts officiated at the ceremony. The bride, who was given away by her father, was attired in a dress of mauve crepe-de-Chine and grey shoes, with hat to match. She carried a bouquet of lilies and roses and was attended by two bridesmaids, Miss Freda Thornton (sister of the bride) and Miss Mildred Kidd

'Milly' (centre back) and friends at Harewood House, near Leeds, 24 May 1950

(sister of the bridegroom) who wore dresses of camelia taffeta silk, with black hats. Their bouquets consisted of gladiolas and irises. The best man was Mr E. Good, of Scarborough. They were the recipients of many presents, amongst which was a very pretty clock, presented by the Scalby Church choir, of which the bridegroom has been a member for 13 years. The happy pair left for Llandudno, where the honeymoon is being spent.

The couple moved to York later, undoubtedly for Henry's employment, possibly with Messrs Leak and Thorpe, of Coney Street, whose original premises dramatically burnt down in January 1933, and were rebuilt on the site over some nine months following demolition of the remains in June of the same year.

Henry, four years older than his sister, outlived Florence, and died suddenly at Scarborough while on a visit from his home at Acomb, near York. His wife it seems, died before him. He left two children, Margaret (born at a York Nursing Home) and David, both of whom married and produced grandchildren – Sally, Alison, Joanna and Philippa.

Florence Mildred Kidd remained at Scalby, living with her mother at 33 North Street, unmarried. As a child 'Milly' first attended the local village school before later entering the roll of Gladstone Road School, Scarborough, 'cycling in each day' recalls Jean Rowntree, daughter of Mrs J.W. Rowntree, and a lifelong friend.

In later life they corresponded frequently and regularly, particularly when Miss Rowntree moved away from Scalby to Kent, while retaining a cottage at Brandsby, and many postcards survive giving a picture of Milly's 'daily round' in old age. Much later, Jean Rowntree was instrumental in assisting Milly gain a place at Ravensworth Lodge, Belgrave Crescent, Scarborough, a residential nursing home owned by the York Friend's

Housing Society, a 'Quaker' organization, and given to them by Joseph Rowntree. But before that time, Milly was most active, even travelling to Switzerland with friends in 1972, while in her seventy-first year of age.

From: Home Farm Cottage, Brandsby, Yorkshire. 2 August 1972

This is a quick one to say that it looks as if we could come over to Scalby on Tuesday 8th. We have been a bit held up because of Anthea, who hasn't long left before she goes back to Australia, but keeps changing her plans. We would look in at the end of the morning. NOT for a meal! But if Tuesday is not convenient, Ben & I could come later, after Mammie [Poore] goes home – we shall be here 2 more weeks. I hope this allows you long enough to let us know. We are in most evenings after 7 (except Monday) if you would rather telephone. Let's hope for better weather.

Best wishes,

Jean R.

From: Home Farm Cottage, Brandsby, Yorkshire. 10 August 1972

This is just to thank you for your hospitality on Tuesday. I do hope you got your own lunch SOMETIME! Also to say how much we enjoyed your Marmalade Ginger bread – I do think it was kind of you to make it – and looking at your cards. Annie asked to be remembered to you & she has a lovely little Jersey cow called Rosie which is quite spoit & wants to be the centre of attention. Its butter, which we had on our bread for tea, was like what we used to have at Low Hall. Next year you must come to Whole Farm in Spring. P.S. I thought this card might interest you.

Best wishes from us all,

Jean R.

The postcard in question was a sepia reproduction of F.M. Sutcliffe's photograph showing corn-ricks being built, entitled, 'The Ingathering'; with a caption stating, 'Taken around 1895 at Four Lane Ends Farm, Whitby. At one time a tollgate was part of the farm through which Bonnie Prince Charlie is reputed to have passed one stormy night.'

From: Chelsea, London. 22 August 1972

Thank you so much for your letter – it was kind of you to keep on writing. In fact Annie rang me the day Tom died – we went to the funeral today – there were so many people you couldn't fit into the chapel, so there was a service outside as well. Annie is going up to Cross Cliff to her sister – it will be the best place as Norah's husband is Tom's brother, & since Daphne got married Norah has been short of company & help. The little cow goes up too! If there is anything about the funeral in any paper you see, I should love to see it as we couldn't quite hear the sermon. We drive south tomorrow.

Best wishes,

Jean R.

From: Ponteland, Northumberland. 24 September 1972

Thank you for your postcard & message. Hope you have enjoyed your visit to Redcar, & all your other visits too. Haven't seen you since Cup Final day with me – Oh! I remember, on a seat opposite the library that day. I've had rather a queer

summer. Cousins with me, then back for a week at Mellor Brook as they had an empty back seat. Betty suggested my going & George brought me back. But I picked up a virus in B'burn [Blackburn?] & became ill after I got home! Better now, & staying up here for a welcome change & good company. I think you will like this sunset view of the Northumberland coast [Beadnell Bay]. It's a lovely county. Hope you are well.
Love from Doris

From: Sheffield, South Yorkshire. 25 October 1972
Dear Aunty Millie,
   Thank you for your letter this week. We shall be coming to Scarborough on Monday 30 October & would like to come & see you. We'll come in the morning, probably about 11. If you will be away or it's not convenient let me know. We shall be having lunch in Scarborough.
love Judy & David, J[oanna] & P[hilippa]

These are brother Henry Kidd's daughter and son-in-law, and their children.

From: Whole Farm, Stone-in-Oxney, Kent. 13 November 1973
   Many thanks for your card – I had a lovely birthday (mostly spent gardening). This is to say that we should like to get you an electric iron for Christmas, but I thought I had better write first to ask if you had one already, & also if you really prefer not to be bothered with it! I think you CAN get the kind where the ironing board plugs in, & you don't have to have a dangling flex on the iron – but I am not sure. Do you remember being hemmed in parking at the place on this card & nearly missing the tram? [High Street, Tenterden, Kent]

From: York. 23 March 1975
   I bought this card at London Zoo. We had a super day and arrived home at 11 pm very tired. The football match was great, England won 4–0. It was a long day, we left York at 6.20 am but it was worth it. Thank you for the postcard.
Love from Alison [Henry Kidd's granddaughter]

From: Home Farm Cottage, Brandsby, Yorkshire. 14 April 1975[?]
   Thank you so much for your letter & the interesting enclosures: I especially like the one about holidays in Scarborough. We were rather late arriving here as I stayed on an extra day in London hoping to see Tony, but there were no trains running & no one could say when there would be, so we had to come up without managing it. This is just to say that we hope to come to Scalby sometime between 22nd & 26th April – AFTER your weekend at David's – I will have to let you know which day later on (it depends on Sarah's plans) but I thought I had better tell you that it won't be this week. I should be very grateful if you could tell me, when we come, if anyone will be taking on Mr Addisons work on the graves, I have an idea that I owe him for last year, & don't know what to do about it? The weather is still pretty miserable but we manage to get out. All news later.
Best wishes,
Jean R.

From: Home Farm Cottage, Brandsby, Yorkshire. 19 April 1975[?]

This is just to ask if Friday (April 25th) would be a possible day for us to look in on you? I have been waiting to hear from Annie Foster, but Norah has shingles very badly & I don't think we ought to go there at all. Not because its catching – it isn't – but because I know from experience how any little exertion or even talking to people can make it worse. However, I do want to see you & talk about plans, & also see the graves. If it is a fine day we should LIKE to go back via Langdale End & get in a walk, so could we look in for a REALLY LIGHT PICNIC LUNCH ABOUT 12.30? NO SPECIAL PREPARATIONS, just an egg and a cup of tea! If you would rather telephone than write, we are always here up to 10am or after 7pm (except on Thursday).

Best wishes,
Jean R.

From: Home Farm Cottage, Brandsby, Yorkshire. 26 April 1975[?]

We went here yesterday [Postcard of Fountains Abbey]. I had forgotten what a lovely place it is. I expect you know it, but we thought we might take you there in August or September for a picnic if you can't come to us in Kent.

It was lovely to see you last week. I thought you looked a bit washed out, and hope your iron tablets will really do you good, & that you won't hesitate to ask your doctor for something stronger (such as iron injections) if you don't feel better quite soon. Meanwhile I am enclosing something to help with the home help. I am sure you won't want to have one permanently. But I think you might find it worth trying for the next few weeks while you are having treatment, & I expect Mrs Lee knows, better than I could, how to set about getting someone.

All Good Wishes,
Jean R.

From: Home Farm Cottage, Brandsby, Yorkshire. 28 April 1975

Before we leave here (first thing tomorrow) I just wanted to thank you for a lovely lunch on Friday. I hope it wasn't too awkward having us the same day as Henry – I wonder how he got on in London? I didn't even see who won the match.*

We also wanted to say that if you don't mind the journey (& the price of travelling) & don't mind not knowing which of the July dates it would be, for a little longer, of course we should really RATHER you got to Whole Farm. It would be more of a change for you. But we should quite understand if you thought it was too much effort & too expensive.

All good wishes from us both. Looking forward to seeing you SOMEWHERE this summer.

Jean R.

*Undoubtedly this postcard reads in connection with one previous (dated 23 March 1975) from Alison, Henry Kidd's granddaughter, who gives the result of the England football match, seen while on a visit to London (Wembley?), obviously with grandad Henry.

From: Whole Farm, Stone-in-Oxney, Kent. 2 May 1975

We got back yesterday – cuckoos singing, and pansies out, but the garden very DRY! We shall have to hoe & water. We found a message, giving us the July dates, waiting & we now see that we shall have no visitors between July 6th & 11th or 12th. The only trouble is that this would mean you travelling on a Saturday – (15th). If you can get a reserved seat it would be alright, & Miss Poore will meet you & put you on the train to Ashford on Sunday (6th). This would mean 5 nights here & you could either go straight through on Friday 11th or spend a night in London & leave on Saturday. I am so sorry we can't fit our visitors so that you could travel mid-week. Let me know sometime what you think.

Best wishes,
Jean R.

From: Whole Farm, Stone-in-Oxney, Kent. 13 May 1975

Thank you so much for your letter. WE should have thanked YOU for a splendid lunch. I have written direct to Mr Addision & hope that is satisfactory. I have also written to Jessie about holiday plans & will let you know when I hear. I have been rather slow about letters as I have had flu & can't seem to shake it off – it has been hanging on for 10 days now & as soon as I feel better & go out it comes back on my chest again. OLD NAMES OF SCALBY ROADS. The only other one I can think of is FOULSYKE (over what used to be the Ford going towards Wrea Head). We have some splendid asparagus & gooseberries & the first roses are out – lovely weather, but we need rain badly. P.S. I have never seen this bay so empty [Postcard of The Bay, Rye].

Best wishes,
Jean R.

From: Whole Farm, Stone-in-Oxney, Kent. 21 June 1975

I have been meaning to write to you ever since I got your letter about the earthquake – however you will realise by now we weren't in it! Though we did in fact feel the tremour when we were going through the Alps in the train that night. We got quite a shaking, & wondered what on earth was happening.

This is one of the places we must take you to see [Chilham Castle] – you can't go round the house, but there is a beautiful garden. It is a very pretty village. We are very much looking forward to seeing you, & I have first had an answer from Jessie, saying that she hopes to be able to get away for a night or two to join us – she is going to try and arrange it & will let me know for certain later. Miss Poore is looking forward to having you on the 20th July – She may not be able to drive you down next day. But she will put you on the train if not. I will write about train times etc early in July.

Best wishes,
Jean R.

From: Whole Farm, Stone-in-Oxney, Kent. 4 July 1975

Thank you so much for your letter. It is good of Henry [Milly's brother] to say he would travel with you to Kings Cross. I have heard from Jessie that she thinks she can manage July 24th–26th, & I expect she would travel back with you on the Monday. The only thing is that unless it gets cooler by then – & surely it must do so soon! – I feel it would be a terribly tiring journey for you, & not even a very good time for a visit. We have Miss Schilling here now – she [was] meant to be here with Mrs Stanley – but Mrs Stanley has a bad heart and isn't allowed to travel in the heat (London is like an oven). She is waiting in the hopes of a break in the weather & is really only able to lie about in the shade & occasionally go to the sea. It is really too hot for picnics. Also we have to spend 2 hours every day, while we are still allowed to, trying to keep our vegetables watered. We have had NO rain since February & the garden is like a desert. Let us hope for a change soon – if not I feel perhaps we ought to postpone your visit for a bit? What do you think?

Best wishes,
Jean R.

From: Home Farm Cottage, Brandsby, Yorkshire. 2 August 1975

I wonder how you are feeling now that the weather has got cooler? We got here this weekend – it has got cooler in the south too, but never a drop of rain yet, & no sign of it – everything spoilt & dried up and no hoses allowed for watering.

What we wondered was if you feel like joining us for a picnic – we could come over with a packed lunch, have a drive somewhere, & tea out, & take you back. We could EITHER do a runner up the coast & back by Harwood Dale OR go to Flamborough for our picnic & on to look at Burton Constable (I am not sure which days it is open to the public) & then put you on a train or bus, say at Seamer or Ayton if you were able to change at Scarborough. I thought I would let you think it over in good time to write. If you would rather write than telephone, our best days would be 9th, 10th or 11th August (Mon, Tues or Wed) but we could probably do Friday 6th if it suited you better. We would come over about 12 or soon after (I want to see Mrs James first) & bring you, or get you back after tea. I hope we can manage something; but not if it would hurt your leg.

Best wishes,
Jean R.

From: Home Farm Cottage, Brandsby, Yorkshire. 10 August 1975

I think we would have looked down on [Lake] Gormire last September, on our way back from Scawton?

This is really to say that, though I am up here for a time, I have to go back to London because of an abscess in a tooth, which means leaving earlier than we had meant. However we are coming back in September (when we should have been abroad) & I know Mary Jones will want to go over to Scalby & Langdale one day, so I thought I should find out if you are likely to be away between September 10th & 20th? I know you were thinking of going to Margaret's sometime. I wonder how your expedition to the Dales went, O.K? & how you are standing this weather – it is a lot hotter here than in Kent – I think the sea cooks us down there. It is all right if you can get on top of the moors or into the sea! We had all the Balmes to their evening meal here on Sarah's birthday – enjoyed it very much until we found we had laid the table (in the garden) at the entrance to a wasps nest. I have Con coming to dinner tonight – she is staying in Haxby.

Best wishes,
Jean R.

From: Home Farm Cottage, Brandsby, Yorkshire. 12 August 1975

Thank you so much for your letter & sending the recipe – I must try it when I bake next. I thought you would like this old view of Rievaulx; I also wanted to tell you a coincidence. We were talking to Ashley yesterday (he comes in for a can of beer and a gossip, & does a very little gardening while he is about it) and we told him where we had been & he said he had been a garden boy (6/- a week) at Burton Constable Hall for years – it was his first job! So he was really interested to hear about your grandparents. Though of course that would be before his time – I think he was there just before the 1914 war. I would love to see your scrapbook sometimes – perhaps when we come up in September. We will let you know in good time. I am sorry you had trouble with the bus. I am afraid you must have got rather tired. We got our meal at 8.45 which was quite good going. We did enjoy the day. Looking forward to another one soon.

Jean R.

From: Cockpit Hall, Gillamoor, Yorkshire. 18 August 1976

Thank you for the money you sent me and Jo. Today we are going to the cinema to see 'It Shouldn't Happen to a Vet'. We have been to Knaresborough and Flamingo Park [Zoo]. On Friday we are going for a picnic in the country. Hope you are well.

Love from Pip & Joanna [Jean Rowntree's niece, Sarah's children]

During late August, it appears Milly took ill, and spent some time in hospital, and from the tone of subsequent letters below, it was from this period that Milly's decline became permanent to the extent that later, it was necessary for her to leave Scalby for a place at Ravensworth Lodge.

From: Home Farm Cottage, Brandsby, Yorkshire. 4 September 1976

We are just packing up for an early start tomorrow, but I thought I would send you a line before we go to say how pleased I was to hear from both Henry & Mrs Lee that they had found you better this week. I think you were ready for a good long rest. If you eat well and get out a bit and don't worry, I am quite sure you will soon be home again, perhaps not at 33 North Street, but at some little place in Scalby where there is almost no work. And don't worry about the clean-up either – there are plenty of people to help – if necessary I would come up for 2 or 3 days myself as I am used to cleaning up, & you would be surprised what things auctioneers will take – your old 'blackout' curtains you were telling me about are just the sort of thing. But do get your name down SOON for a bungalow. I asked our friend Kate Mahoney to let us know how you are & if there is anything you want. All good wishes for your complete recovery.

Jean R.

From: Whole Farm, Stone-in-Oxney, Kent. 5 September 1976

I have just heard from Jessie, who would like to come for two nights between Sept 26 & Oct 5th, so we have looked at our dates again – we have 2 guests on October 5th, & Miss S is away until Sept 26th, but if you could travel to London for the night of Sept 27th, Miss Poore could probably drive you down on 28th & you could get back to London on October 4th, & travel back on the 5th – is this possible? I know Jessie would be very disappointed not to see you – but I hope this notice is not too short. We got here Monday – my car failed on the motorway & is off for a week at least. I have Trust meetings in York the weekend of September 14th so could you let me know HERE if possible by return, to catch me before I leave?

Best wishes,
Jean R.

From: Whole Farm, Stone-in-Oxney, Kent. 17 September 1976

This is one of the houses we never went to with you, I think? [Batemans, Burwash, Sussex: Rudyard Kipling's home from 1902–36, now a National Trust property.] We must try to do it next time you come here. It is a lovely place, where Kipling wrote most of his books.

I am writing now to say that, unless you hear to the contrary, Miss Poore & I will call for you on Saturday afternoon – could you be ready about 2 o'clock? Then I thought we could drive to Whitby for some fish for our meal from the pier, have a look at the sea, & come back by Rosedale & Lastingham. It is a beautiful drive. If you want to make any alterations, I shall be at BRANDSBY 229 by Friday evening – I am not sure how long the Trust will go on, but I ought to be back by 6 o'clock. Bring old clothes – we might pick blackberries! & let us hope for good weather. Looking forward to seeing you.

Jean R.

From: Whole Farm, Stone-in-Oxney, Kent. 20 September 1976

This is just a note to let you know that we shall be coming to the cottage at the end of next week, when I have a Trust meeting in York, & wondered if – weather permitting – you would like to come for a picnic with us on September 29th – or 30th (Wed or Thurs)? We thought of going up the coast, & having a picnic near Boggle Hole & tea in Whitby. We shall be at the cottage from Sept 24 on, so it would be safer to write there – we are well, but I have cracked a joint & have frozen shoulder. Am spending HOURS at the physiotherapist. However we have had good rainings, so no more watering is needed & the garden is looking to itself again.

Jean R.

From: Borrowdale, Cumbria. 6 October 1976[?]

We got home safely last week, but had to turn back twice to find another route because of floods. Several cars were stuck in *water* and abandoned. I have enjoyed reading the scrapbook – it is really your family scrapbook as well as your Granny's & I think I ought to post it back to you when I get back to the cottage – you won't want to be without it till January. We had a lovely drive here on Monday – sunny all the way to Kirkby Stephen, when it clouded over & got wet. We came by Swaledale, which we didn't know, & thought it was one of the most beautiful of the dales; quite unspoilt country. Yesterday we got up to the top of a pass in fine weather. Then it came on to rain & we had to come down & dry up. We did enjoy seeing you last week.

Best wishes,
Jean R.

From: Whole Farm, Stone-in-Oxney, Kent. 8 October [?]

You will remember seeing this garden? [Sissinghurst Castle] This is just to say that I have heard from Dr Goulder, who says you can't get treatment at the hospital & have to have it done privately. Let him know (or rather, let *me* know) & he will write a letter for you to give to the physiotherapist. I hope you had a lovely time in Harrogate. I wonder if you got to Haworth? I had the beautiful September weather here.

All good wishes,
Jean R.

From: 30 Glebe Place, Chelsea, London SW3.

Thank you for such a nice letter & your sympathy over my horrid burglary. The mess was awful – This was the only one where they took everything of antique value as well as precious things of no value. I am so sorry you have been feeling your illnesses so much more this winter & it must be depressing. I do hope some more physiotherapy may help. It will be lovely your coming in the summer with your brother. I was down [in Kent] for 2 nights last weekend & the place was lovely in spring flowers & the woods full of promises. Jean & Ben were well – I was sorry about Jemi too, but she seems to be going on well. The quack told me she has been very ill with heart trouble – she is better but must rest a lot & must not garden any more.

Mammie P.

From: Chelsea, London.

I am looking forward to seeing you on Thursday. If you let me know the time you arrive I will arrange for a car to meet you at Kings Cross. I think Amy may like to come and meet you. I unfortunately teach until 4, but hope to be free by the time you get to Glebe Place. I shan't be able to drive you down on Friday but will see that you are taken to the station on Friday afternoon. This will give you a morning to look at Chelsea antique shops, & we can arrange about a theatre for the following Thursday night – which I shall look forward to – with love Mammie Poore. PS. I am afraid I have not left you much time to reply, so I suggest that we meet the 3.34 at Kings X leaving Scarboro' 10.50, unless you let me know to the contrary.

From: Whole Farm, Stone-in-Oxney, Kent. 5 February 1977[?]

I have just got your letter & want to get this off at once, so I haven't time to go to look at gas stoves, but Miss Poore has just arrived – (she has a nasty chest cold, & has come here for four days to be looked after & keep warm). She says she thinks you ought to ask at the gas showroom for a stove which is also a *CONVECTOR*, as this spreads the heat more evenly all over the room. I hope they will put it in quickly – (then of course the weather will change). We must have a picnic on the cliffs next time you come. I am so glad Henry's ulcer is better – he must take care not to go too long without food. It is enough if you just suck a Horlicks malted milk tablet (my doctor gave me them). I never heard of anyone going to Turkey for a *week* – how people do get about now!

Jean R.

From: Whole Farm, Stone-in-Oxney, Kent. 12 February 1977[?]

Thank you so much for your letter and for sending the illustration. Let me know if you want it back. It is so long since I bought a gas fire (at £5!) that I had forgotten how expensive they would be – I wanted to get something to you quickly, and didn't have a chance to ask at a shop. So here is the [ ] which I hope is right – I do want to give you the whole thing because, with everything costing so much, it is quite a big item. It looks just like the kind I hoped you would get, as it heats the whole room, not just a bit of it. It is more like spring here – tea by daylight, snowdrops & crocusses out. We have Anthea's daughter [Jean R's sister's child] coming for the weekend, & Con [Jean R's sister] the week after.

All good wishes,
Jean R.

From: Whole Farm, Stone-in-Oxney, Kent. 15 February 1977[?]

We were so glad to hear from you. I had been meaning to write to say we had to put off coming to Brandsby. No, were are not flooded – this house, of course, is on a ridge, & the river below has been well drained lately. There were floods on some roads, but they have gone more or less now; but we did have tremendous gales – my gardening basket was blown away & I nearly went with it.

I had hoped to get to Brandsby this month or last, but my ill friend is still living, though getting weaker every day, & she does so love having short visits, and I can still go over (120 miles both ways) for 15 minutes once a week, & I can still get the peaches – at a price. Also Tony badly needs a rest & may come here if Sarah [Jean R's niece] can get away to look after Mammie – we don't *know when* this will be, because Sarah's matron has walked out, & they have a flu epidemic! So it doesn't look as if we could leave until April. We will certainly go then, if there is any petrol by that time. I will let you know.

Best wishes,
Jean R.

By early- to mid-1978, Milly Kidd was a permanent resident at Ravensworth Lodge, Scarborough, where she remained until her death in 1979. The staff recall Milly as a kindly, generous person and remember her with affection. Her obituary in the *Scarborough Evening News* was brief:

On November 30, 1979, in hospital, Florence Mildred Kidd, aged 78 years (late of 33 North Street and Ravensworth Lodge) greatly loved sister of Henry Kidd and

A gold-foil chocolate wrapper pasted into the Kidd family album, presented to schoolchildren at the time of Queen Victoria's Diamond Jubilee

dear aunt of Margaret and David. Service at St Lawrence's church, Scalby, on Thursday (6 December) at 11.15 am followed by private cremation.

With the death of Milly, the family album, so lovingly filled by three generations, appears to have ceased. Among the pages still however, further to those family references previously noted, are many others – wedding and birth notices, celebration pieces, and more obituaries – of various other members of the Kidd family, persons familiar to those in Scalby, and for that reason, a number are reproduced here in conclusion:

December 1927: The remains of the late Mr Thomas Harland, Grange-lane, North Ferriby, were laid to rest in All Saint's Churchyard on Monday afternoon. The deceased, who was 52 years of age, was taken ill on Monday week, and died in the early hours of Friday morning from pneumonia. He was greatly respected and universally liked, being ever ready to help anybody. He was appointed the first hon. secretary of the North Ferriby Horticultural and Sports Society when it was restarted and had held that office for about eight years. He was also a member of the North Ferriby Branch of the British Legion. Much sympathy is felt for his widow and daughter and son. The service was conducted by the vicar (the Rev. R. Harris Lloyd), and the chief mourners were, Mrs Harland (widow), Mr F. Harland (son), Miss M. Harland (daughter), Mrs Pickering (sister), **Mrs Kidd** (sister-in-law), Miss Abram (sister-in-law), Mr J. Tindall (nephew), Mr & Mrs Willings . . .

Tindall.– On November 7th, at Home Farm, Scalby, Esther Margaret aged 83 years, widow of Edwin Tindall, late of Harwood Dale. Interment at Scalby, Friday, November 10th [1944]. Service in the Wesleyan Chapel at 2.30pm.

QUEEN'S DIAMOND JUBILEE.

The Mayor of Middlesbrough's (Colonel Sadler) Celebrations.

WORDS TO BE SUNG

By the Sunday School Scholars, at the Demonstration in the Albert Park,

On TUESDAY, the 22nd day of JUNE, 1897.

The Bands will play the first Verse of each before the Singing commences, and three Beats will be given on the Drum before the first and between each verse.

CONDUCTOR   ...   ...   WILLIAM BLENKINSOP.

No. 1. Rule Britannia.

M. 60.   *Key B♭.*

Bands play the First Verse.

Three beats on Drum.

When Britain first at heaven's command
   Arose from out the azure main,
This was the charter of the land,
   And guardian angels sang this strain.

CHORUS SUNG TWICE :—
   Rule Britannia! Britannia rules the waves,
   Britons never will be slaves.

Three beats on Drum.

   The nations not so blest as thee,
     Must in their turn to tyrants fall ;
   Whilst thou shalt flourish great and free,
     The dread and envy of them all.

CHORUS :—Rule Britannia, etc.

Three beats on Drum.

   To thee belongs the rural reign,
     · Thy cities shall with commerce shine ;
 · All thine shall be the subject main,
     And every shore it circles thine !

CHORUS :—Rule Britannia, etc.

Three beats on Drum.

   The Muses ! still with freedom found,
     Shall to thy happy coast repair ;
   Blest isle ! with matchless beauty crown'd
     And manly hearts to guard the fair.

CHORUS :—Rule Britannia, etc.

No. 2. National Anthem.

M. 72.   *Key A.*

Bands play the First Verse.

Three beats on Drum.

God save our gracious Queen,
   Long live our noble Queen,
     God save the Queen !
Send her victorious,
Happy and glorious,
Long to reign over us,
   God save the Queen.

Three beats on Drum.

   Crowned by a nation's love,
   Guarded by heaven above,
     Long live the Queen !
Loud may each voice proclaim,
Wi a Britannia's fame,
Long live Victoria's name,
   God save the Queen !

Three beats on Drum.

   God bless our native land,
   May heaven's protecting hand,
     Still guard our shore ;
   May peace her power extend,
   Foe be transformed to friend,
   And Britain's rights depend,
     On war no more.

Three beats on Drum.

   God save our gracious Queen,
   Long live our noble Queen,
     God save the Queen !
Send her victorious,
Happy and glorious,
Long to reign over us,
   God save the Queen !

A programme of events attended by schoolchildren held in Albert Park, Middlesbrough

The funeral of Mrs E. Tindall took place at Scalby on Friday afternoon. Prior to the interment a service was held at the methodist Chapel. The Rev. R.G. Pittam conducted the service. The principal mourners were, Mr and Mrs F. Tindall (son and daughter-in-law), Mr and Mrs J.P. Tindall (son and daughter-in-law), Mr H. Tindall (grandson), **Mrs M. Kidd**, Mrs Willings, Mrs Ward, Mrs Barker (sisters), Mr F. Abram (brother), Mr F. Willings, Mr J. Ward, Mr Barker (brothers-in-law), **Miss M. Kidd**, Mr and Mrs A. Kneeshaw, Mr and Miss Jackson (nephews and nieces). A wreath was sent from the Methodist Chapel, Harwood Dale.

Obituary.– The interment of Thomas Edward John Fenwick, of The Park, Scalby, who died suddenly on Friday morning of last week, took place at Scalby on Tuesday afternoon. The service was conducted by the Rev. H.M. Tapper in the absence of the vicar. Deceased, who was 76 years of age, had resided at Scalby for 16 years. There was a large attendance of friends present at the churchyard. Among the chief mourners were **Mr and Mrs Kidd**, who sent a floral tribute also.

January 31, 1937. Burniston lost an old and respected resident on Sunday in the death of Mrs Mary Jane Kneeshaw at the age of 74. Mrs Kneeshaw and her husband celebrated their golden wedding in November last. Mrs Kneeshaw was the third daughter of the late Mr F. Abram, of Burniston. The interment took place on Tuesday, and was preceded by a service in Burniston Methodist Church conducted by Mr R. Frankish. Deceased had been a member of the church for the past 40 years, and a short appreciative address was given by Mr Frankish. There was a large attendance at church. The hymns sung were 'O God our help', and 'Lead kindly light'. The interment took place at Scalby, and the service at the graveside was conducted by the vicar of Scalby. Chief mourners were: Mr W. Kneeshaw (widower), Mrs Postgate (daughter), from Barnsley, Mr and Mrs A. Kneeshaw (son and daughter-in-law), from Barnsley; the eldest son was unable to be present through indisposition; Mr and Mrs J. Crawford (sister and brother-in-law), **Mr and Mrs Edwin Kidd** (sister and brother-in-law), Mr and Mrs Ward (sister and brother-in-law), Mr and Mrs F. Abram (brother and sister-in-law), and a number of nephews and nieces. The numerous floral tributes included one from the Burniston Chapel.

March 1940. A Scarborough couple, Mr and Mrs John Crawford, of 24 Sherwood Street, who, during the weekend celebrated the golden anniversary of their wedding, are related to the Mayor and Mayoress. Mr Crawford is the brother of the Mayoress.

He is 74 years of age and his wife is 76. They were married at St Mary's Parish Church on March 8th, 1890. Until his retirement about 20 years ago, Mr Crawford was caretaker of Gladstone Road Schools. He takes a keen interest in cricket, and has followed local and county matches for many years. Before her marriage Mrs Crawford was Miss Rachel Abram, of Clarence House, Burniston. Mr and Mrs Crawford are members of the Methodist Church and have long been regular attenders at the Queen Street Central Hall.

They have one son and one daughter – Sub-Inspector J.E. Crawford, of the North Riding Police, who is stationed at Thirsk, and Mrs H. Pearson, of Ashington, Northumberland. Another daughter, Mrs Hanford, wife of Mr R.A. Hanford,

SCALBY CHURCH ORGAN FUND.

LIST OF SUBSCRIPTIONS.

	£	s.	d.
Mr. and Mrs. Tingle-Brown, Scalby	25	0	0
Mr. and Mrs. Howgate, „	15	0	0
Mr. and Mrs. Huggan, „	15	0	0
Capt. and Mrs. Clarke, „	2	2	0
Mr. and Miss Nicholls, „	2	2	0
Lady Sitwell (1st don.) „	10	0	0
Mrs. Green, Boston Spa ..	2	0	0
Miss Green, Scarborough	2	0	0
Lord Derwent, Hackness	5	5	0
Miss E. P. Hebden, Scarborough	1	1	0
Mr. W. Rhodes, Leeds	10	0	0
Mrs. Cox, Scarborough	10	10	0
Mrs. Cooke, Leamington	2	0	0
Mrs. Magson, Scarborough	5	0	0
Rev. W. and Mrs. Cautley-Robinson, Scalby	5	0	0
M.E. late „	2	0	0
A Summer Visitor (per Mrs. Tingle-Brown)	5	0	0
Mr. and Mrs. J. W. Booth (1st donation) Scalby	2	2	0
Mrs. J. W. Rowntree, „	5	0	0
Mr. John Gibson, „	1	0	0
Mr. John Robinson, „	0	10	0
Mrs. Coates, „	3	0	0
Miss Ward, „	1	1	0
Mr. Edward Barker's Concert	6	0	0
Mr. and Mrs. Edward Barker, Scalby	4	0	0
Mr. J. P. Boddy, „	1	1	0
Mr. J. Thompson-Pegge, „	2	2	0
Mrs. Donner, Cloughton	3	3	0
Mr. W. S. Wright (1st don.) Scalby	10	0	0
Mr. Edward Wallis, Scarboro'	1	1	0
Mr. and Mrs. Ashby, „	2	2	0
Mr. Straw, Scalby	5	0	0
Mrs. Muil „	2	2	0
Colonel Howard „	1	1	0
Mr. Hutton „	0	10	6
Messrs. Wallis & Blakeley „	2	2	0
Dr. and Mrs. Grummitt „	2	2	0
Mr. Leonard Thompson „	0	10	6
Mr. F. Murgatroyd „	0	10	6
Mrs. Clough „	1	1	0
Mrs. Ellen Marsden, Sheffield	1	1	0
Major C. Fox, J.P., Dewsbury	10	0	0
Mr. Duke Fox, J.P. „	5	0	0
Mr. Wm. Sykes, Starbeck	5	0	0
Mr. W. E. Leadley, Burniston	0	10	0
Mrs. Hodgson „	0	10	0

	£	s.	d.
Mrs. March, Scalby	5	0	0
Miss March, Leeds	5	5	0
Mr. J. Challinor, Leek	1	10	6
Gervase Beckett, Esq., M.P. ..	2	2	0
Rev. The Marquis of Normanby	3	3	0
Mrs. Colton-Fox, Harrogate	1	0	0
A Friend (per Mrs. Howgate)	1	1	0
Mrs. Harrison, Burniston	0	15	0
Mr. J. Harrison „	0	5	0
E.L.S., Sheffield (per Mrs. Tingle-Brown)	1	1	0
Mrs. Berry, Scalby	2	2	0
Mr. Lotinga „	1	1	0
Mrs. Abram „	0	5	0
Mr. Sam Smithson, Heckmondwike	1	1	0
Sir Edward Donner, Bart., Manchester	5	0	0
Mrs. D. Cautley, Harrogate	5	0	0
Rev. Chas. Johnstone, Hackness	3	0	0
Mr. Joe Ramsden, Birstall	1	1	0
Mr. and Mrs. T. Tasker Hart, Scalby	1	1	0
Lady Sitwell (2nd don.) „	10	0	0
Mr. Isaac Noble „	0	10	0
Mr. W. H. Stonehouse, Newby	0	10	0
Mr. Geo. Dixon, Scalby	5	0	0
Miss Tong, Eriswell	0	10	0
Rev. L. S. Robinson, Bingley	1	1	0
Dr. Hammond, Scalby	1	0	0
Mrs. Cattley (1st don.) „	5	0	0
Mr. and Mrs. Claridge „	2	2	0
Miss Alice Adams „	0	10	0
Mr. and Mrs. Forest Hall „	1	1	0
A Member of the Congregation „	200	0	0
Mrs. Power „	0	10	0
Mrs. Steele „	0	10	0
M.B. „	1	0	0
Miss Kirby, Newby	0	5	0
Mrs. Gabb „	1	1	0
Mr. and Mrs. Heaton „	0	10	6
Mr. George Bradley, Scarboro'	0	5	0
Dr. Howgate, Worcester	0	5	0
Mrs. C. Leng, Scalby	0	2	6
Mrs. Farndale „	0	10	0
Miss E. M. Hart „	0	10	0
Miss Lizzie Hodgson „	0	10	0
Miss Wade „	0	2	6
Mr. John Gibson Leadley, Burniston	0	10	0
Mr. Emmerson Ward „	1	0	0

	£	s.	d.
Mr. George Rowntree, Scarbro'	0	5	0
Mrs. S. W. Rice, „	0	10	0
Miss Beetham „	0	10	0
Mr. W. S. Rowntree „	0	10	0
Mr. & Mrs. Hardcastle, Scalby	5	0	0
Mr. H. E. Douner, Cloughton	1	1	0
Mr. and Mrs. Jones, Scalby	1	1	0
Per Mrs. Kidd—	£	s.	d.
Rev. Dr. and Mrs. Morton, Whitfield Rectory	1	0	0
Mr. T. P. Cooke, Olton, Birmingham	1	0	0
Miss Ellison, Lincoln	0	3	0
Miss Coombs, Bath	0	2	0
Churchwoman, Scalby	0	5	0
Mr. I. Watson „	0	1	0
Mr. I.P.B. „	0	1	0
L.L.T. „	0	0	6
Mr. and Mrs. Edwin Kidd, Summerhill	0	2	6
Miss Kidd, Scalby	0	2	6
Mrs. Kidd „	0	2	6
	3	0	0
Mrs. Hoyle, Scarborough	1	0	0
Mrs. Forest Hall (collected) Scalby	2	2	0
Mr. and Mrs. I. Cockerill, Burniston	0	10	0
Mr. F. Harrison „	0	10	6
Mrs. Rhodes, Newby	0	10	0
H.P. Scarborough	0	2	6
Exors. of the late E. L. Donner, Cloughton	5	5	0
Messrs. Gibson Bros., Scalby	1	0	0
Mrs. Challinor „	1	0	0
Mrs. Cattley (2nd don.) „	5	0	0
Mr. J. C. Turton „	2	2	0
Mr. John Ashton „	0	10	0
Mr. and Mrs. J. W. Booth (2nd don.) „	1	1	0
Miss Cromack „	0	10	0
Messrs. G. F. Smith & Son ..	0	5	0
Mr. and Mrs. Bray, Scalby Hall	25	0	0
Mr. W. S. Wright (2nd don.) Scalby	3	2	1
	£540	0	

Inspector of Taxes, Manchester, died about thirteen years ago. There are two grand-daughters, the Misses Hanford.

The Mayor and Mayoress attended the party in celebration of the anniversary, and **Mr Edwin Kidd**, of Curraghmore Terrace, Scalby, who was the best man at their wedding, also attended. But for indisposition, Mrs J. Ward of Castle Road, who was the bridesmaid, would also have been present.

November 20, 1955. The death took place on Sunday of Mr Fred Willings, a retired gardener, of 13 Coldyhill Lane, Newby. He was 66. A native of East Lutton, Mr Willings came to Scalby in 1921, where he was employed as a chauffeur and gardener. He was a member of North Street Chapel, Scalby, and during the war years was employed as a special constable. He is survived by his widow and son.

A funeral service at North Street Chapel, Scalby on Wednesday, was conducted by the Rev. Percy Jackson, the organist being Mr Jenkinson.

The chief mourners were Mrs Emily Cecilia Willings (widow) Mr and Mrs G.A. Willings (son and daughter-in-law), Mrs G.S. Day and Miss B. Merryweather (sister and niece), Mr and Mrs C. Anderson (niece and husband), Miss E.A. Abram and Mrs Ward (sisters-in-law), **Mr and Miss Kidd**, Mr and Mrs Kneeshaw, Mr and Mrs J.P. Tindall (nephews and nieces). Mr Tom Willings (brother) was unable to attend owing to illness.

Other mourners included: Mr and Mrs P. Thompson, Miss E. Stephenson, Mrs Stenton, and numerous friends from the district.

CHAPTER SEVEN

Marriage Lines

In the days before television and the 'soap-opera', even before the advent of radio and *The Archers*, people took their social amusements and roles from the antics of their peers and the 'doings' of their social 'betters'. The village was then a much more tight-knit community, deriving strength and comfort from a 'closeness' between master and servant, employer and employee – villagers, in the widest sense, shared and cared together.

At the death of Lord Derwent, when the remains of the baron were laid to rest 'beneath the shadow of the quaint old church of St Hilda at Hackness', the coffin bearers 'were old servants, Stone, the butler, and Lord Derwent's valet, Murray, among them'.

In wills too, it was not unusual to find faithful retainers rewarded with a bequest. The late Lord Airedale, latterly of Gledhow Hall, Leeds, and for whom Henry Kidd worked when he lived at Cober Hill, Cloughton, left on his death, over one million pounds, of which the butler, Bartholomew O'Gorman received £500; William Grix, the gardener £250; Rebecca and Sarah Denison, two laundrymaids, £250 each; and Wood, the coachman, £100. 'Also, to each indoor and outdoor servant at Gledhow Hall who [had] been in service two complete years, excepting those just mentioned who have legacies', Lord Airedale left 'a sum equal to one year's wages'.

In response, the servant rewarded the master with hard work, loyalty and a devotion almost beyond duty, and at times of festivities – weddings for instance – they, and the village, would respond with an overwhelming generosity. It was also such occasions that provided the 'meat' against the daily grind, when the 'village' could blossom and relax.

At Scalby Holt, Mr James A. Cooke, proprietor of the *Hull Daily* and *Weekly News* once lived with his wife, son and daughter. On the occasion of his son's 'coming-of-age' at twenty-one:

the whole of the staff of the two journals was very kindly invited by Mr and Mrs Cooke to share in the rejoicings incident to the event, and on [the] Monday morning, between forty and fifty of the employees travelled to Scarborough. Fortunately, the weather had taken a change for the better upon that of the previous day, and the Scarborough experiences of the visitors [from Hull] both in this respect and in the welcome they received at Scalby Holt, were of a very pleasant and thoroughly enjoyable character.

Scalby Holt, the residence of Mr Cooke, is picturesquely situated about two or three miles out of Scarborough, and on the arrival of the staff at Scarborough they were conveyed to Scalby by conveyances very thoughtfully placed at their disposal. The welcome extended to each by Mr and Mrs Cooke placed everybody *bon accord*, and a stroll through the compact and beautiful grounds attached to the mansion brought round the hour which every Englishman, with appetite sharpened by crisp sea breezes, anticipates with dear delight, whether at home or abroad.

The sounds of the 'tom-tom' sent everyone flocking into a very comfortable and commodious tent. Covers had been laid for about 70, and this number was made up by a number of ladies and gentlemen, friends of the family. Every justice was done to the thoroughly English dinner which was served up, and at the close Mr Cooke, who of course presided, called upon the company to honour as loyal Englishmen, the health of her Gracious Majesty the Queen. No one was backward in the rendition of this Tribute to the Throne, and then came what was admittedly the feature of the afternoon's proceedings. This was the presentation of a congratulatory address from the staff of the *Hull News* to Mr T. Percy Cooke on the attainment of his majority.

Mr S.O. Cawthorne, the manager of the establishment, undertook the reading of the address, and discharged the duty well, although visibly moved by the many past scenes which doubtless came within his mind's eye – reminiscences of nearly forty years' connections with the *Hull News*. Dr Wright of Scarborough, next proposed the health of Mr Percy Cooke, and a very appropriate reply was made by that gentleman, both to the address and to the sentiment of his health, which was enthusiastically honoured by the company. Mr R.S. Pickering, the editor of the *Hull News*, proposed the health of Mr and Mrs Cooke in felicitous terms, and the company made the acknowledgement musically, and with ringing cheers. Mr Cooke briefly replied.

Only one toast was now left that of the ladies, and Mr Prissick, the oldest employee, was selected to do duty for the fair sex. The old gentleman however, was too full of his recollections of past struggles and triumphs to enter heartily into the theme which had been given him, and the result was that the ladies fared rather ill at his hands. However, the whole proceedings were thoroughly successful, and afforded, amongst other things, a practical proof of the popularity the proprietor and his family enjoy among the staff.

The visitors were still further entertained at tea during the evening, and departed to catch the last train for Hull with lively recollections of a day well spent and unmistakably enjoyable from the commencement to the close of the visit. Some very valuable presents were received by Mr Percy Cooke from friends, in honour of the attainment of his majority.

When, a number of years later, Thomas Percy Cooke, BA. barrister-at-law, took as his bride Clara Mabel, second daughter of R. Rudgard, of The Hall, Scalby, the day after:

Thursday, the entire number of villagers, some six or seven hundred, were entertained in the Hall park. All manner of sports were on the programme, and the competition was both keen and enjoyable. Long tables were [then] spread under the trees, where the entire company sat down to a sumptuous tea. Jollity reigned and kindly expressions for the welfare of the couple were heard on every side.

On the wedding day previous, the village was reported as 'en fete'. Never before in the history of the oldest inhabitant had there been such a gathering of villagers and townsfolk in and about the church. From the door to the churchyard gates, and away into the street, were congregated groups of disappointed spectators; while inside, the church was taxed to its utmost limits. The grey, time-worn, old edifice, gaily decorated with greenery, flowers and bunting, seemed as though it had entered into the spirit of the joyous occasion:

Especially pleasing was it to see the number of cherry-cheeked children among the concourse of well-wishers. Both the bride and bridegroom have established themselves in the hearts of Scalby. The former as a Sunday School teacher and visitor has made many youthful friends; while Mr Cooke, as a good all-round cricketer, and as one who has entered into all forms of sports, has collected around himself a vast host of admirers and well-wishers. Both families are universally respected and beloved, and the marriage was a popular one. What more need be said of the enthusiasm in the village?

Scalby was dressed in its best; little white frocks, pink and blue sashes, with captivating hoods and bonnets, darted in and out, jostling each other laughingly as they stood about the church. The ceremony was to take place at half-past two, but two hours before that time the streets were filled, and carriages and dog-carts, horses and cycles, were arriving every moment.

Bunting was displayed in the village. The red ensign floated from the church tower, while other national flags lined the route from the Hall. Along the bridal path from the street to the church door a crimson royal carpet was laid. The clouds which had been threatening cleared off, and the sun shone brightly at the appointed hour. The bells were pealing merrily when the bride, leaning on her father's arm, arrived. Inside the decorators had been busy at work. Taste had guided their efforts, and the result was charming. Festoons of flowers hung from every conceivable projection, falling in graceful curves or winding their way around the solid stone pillars.

Following the ceremony, a pretty sight, indeed, was the bridal procession as it left the church. The bride carried a large bouquet of orchids, which fell in a graceful flowering pendant from the centre. The bouquets of the bridesmaids were equally as large, and consisted of pink roses in keeping with those worn in their hats. The scholars of the village day and Sunday schools lined the route as far as the gate, and threw a wealth of floral tributes on the path. The happy couple left by train for Newcastle, from which place they intended proceeding to the banks of the Tweed for their honeymoon.

After the wedding, when the bridal party had returned to Scalby Hall where a large number of personal friends of the bride and bridegroom's families sat down to breakfast, it was reported:

The happy couple were the recipients of some hundreds of handsome presents from friends and well-wishers all over the kingdom. Massive plate, ornaments of the most chaste and unique description, valuable pictures, articles of furniture, vases, and nick-nacks of all kinds, were spread in glorious array for the sight of privileged visitors to Scalby Hall. Long tables and short ones filled not one large room but three. But chief amongst all these were sundry gifts which were pointed to with especial pride – the presents made to the bride by her Sunday school class, the teachers of the village day school, and by the members of the choir; and to the bridegroom by the Scalby cricket club, and by the employees of the *Hull News*, of which paper Mr Cooke, senior is proprietor.

The list was then given in its entirety, and was extensive, even exhaustive, but bears repeating if only to provide a picture of the esteem with which the village held their social 'betters', and as a social document to the customs of the time.

From the bridegroom to the bride, an enamel heart pendant set with pearls and diamonds, and a silver flask; from the bride to the bridegroom, a set of pearl studs; bride's mother, a piano, pictures, silver-backed brush and comb, house linen, Chippendale china, &c; bride's father, chest of silver-plate; bridegroom's mother, silver-mounted cut-glass scent bottle, handsome silver tea service, grandfather clock, &c; bridegroom's father to bride, a diamond heart pendant with pearl and gold chain; to bridegroom, furniture, &c; Miss Rudgard (sister of the bride), silver hand lamp; Miss Ethel and Olive Rudgard, Dresden china clock and picture; the Revd R.W. Rudgard, salt and pepperettes, and prayer and hymn book combined; Miss A.H. Rudgard and Mr E.H. Rudgard, silver and buck horn mounted carvers; Mr W. Rudgard, Derby dessert service; Mrs Rudgard, Wedgewood dessert salad bowl; Mr and Mrs Frank Stone, silver tea tray; Mrs C. Little, sugar dredger; Mr and Mrs Arch Jackson, silver fish knives and forks; Mrs Gelston, silver stamp box; Mr and Mrs Lockwood, sugar bowl and spoon; Mr John E. Ellis, MP, and Mrs Ellis, two dessert spoons; Dr and Mrs Jones, entrée and breakfast dish; Lieut.-Col., Mrs and Miss Steble, silver candlestick; Major and Mrs Smirthwaite, silver salver; Mr and Mrs T. Cooke, silver tea service; Mr F.S. Jackson, cut-glass scent bottle; Revd and Mrs D'Arcy Morton (bridegroom's brother-in-law), sugar basin; Revd and Mrs G. Robinson, gong; Mr and Mrs J.E. Marsden, brass hanging lamp; Mr H.J. Marsden, silver cigarette case; Mr Charles Saner, silver cake knife; Mr and Mrs Grotrian, silver sweetmeat dishes; Mr and Mrs Goddard, silver dessert spoons; Mr C.H.O. Saner, silver cake basket; Mr Albert Saner, silver mounted claret jug; Mr and Mrs James Woodhouse, silver candlesticks; Dr and Mrs E. Taylor, silver butter dish; Mr and Mrs George Hudson, silver pepperette; Mr and Mrs Baker, silver tea caddy; Misses Baker and Mr and Mrs C. Baker, silver fruit spoon; Mr and Mrs John Dale, silver salt cellar; Mr, Mrs and Miss Drawbridge, silver antique spoon; Mr Donner, copper fern bowl; Dr and Mrs Hudson, silver cream and sugar stand; Mr and Miss Wharton, silver cream gatherer; Miss Lees and Miss Thompson, silver trinket holder; Mr and Mrs Brogden, silver pepperette; Dr and Mrs Teal, silver sugar sifter; Mrs Cooper, writing case; Miss Cooper, silver bell; Mrs John and Mr R. Kitchen, silver salt cellars; Mr and Mrs Micheiston, cut-glass scent bottle; Miss Taylor, gold brooch; Mr and Mrs Daniel, gold bracelet; Miss Moore, silver pin tray; Miss Watcher, silver mirror; Miss Green, silver preserve stand; Misses Brigge, silver bread platter and knife; Mrs and Misses Terry, bronze candlesticks; Dr and Mrs Wright, silver coffee pot; Mrs Spoor, silver toast rack; Mr and Mrs Peckham, pearl mounted lace fan; Miss Kirke, antique soup plates; Major Broadrick, silver teapot; Mr J.H. and Miss Robson, silver pickle fork; Mr W.F.D. Smith, silver sweetmeat dishes; Miss Ann Jackson, silver toast rack; Mr A. Jackson, serviette ring; Mrs Kent, silver pepperette; Revd George Kent, silver mounted gum bottle; Mr and Mrs T.C. Bourne, silver serviette ring; Mr and Mrs C.

Walker, silver salt cellars; Mr and Mrs A. Jameson, silver cream jug; Mr H. Ostler and Mr H. Grotrian, silver sweetmeat dishes; Mr and Mrs Hoyle, silver bread fork; Martin Hoyle, silver mounted paper knife; Mr W.W. Hall, serviette rings; Miss B. Buckly, silver apostle teaspoons; Mr Atkinson, silver hot-water jug; Mr John Simmonds, silver hot-water jug; Mr and Mrs Brooke, silver candlesticks; Mrs Ford, Minton china inkstand; Mrs Loy, silver mustard pot; Mr J. Bilson, silver cream jug; Mrs Merry, silver mustard pot; Mrs Ostler, Indian lace handkerchief; Mr and Mrs H. Little, ditto; Miss and Mrs Terry, *point-de-riennese*; Miss Brook, silver clock; Misses M. and W. Chatham, silver paper knife; Mr John Saner, silver pepperettes; Dr and Mrs Massey, silver salt cellars; Mr N. Morton, Miss C. Ford, pearl and diamond brooch; Mr and Mr C.N. Jackson, silver tobacco jar; Mrs Green, specimen vases; Miss Thompson, silver butter knife; Mr H. Little, Hungarian vases; Mr Lathbury, brass umbrella stand; Mr Pierce, bookstand; Mr and Mrs Geo. Bohns, bronze tray; Herr and Frau Ramann, Bohemian china tray and glasses; Mrs Smith, silver sugar tongs and tablecloths; Mr H. Morton, picture; Miss S. Barker, china vase; Mrs Albert Barker, coffee set; Miss Boden, china cake basket; Mrs M. Moore, china vases; Mr and Mrs Hardcastle, brass letter rack; Miss Lucy Lockwood, china coffee set; Mr Botterill, Chippendale caddy and tray; Mr and Mrs G. Taylor, china cake basket; Mr, Mrs and the Misses Cawthorne, china tea service; Mr and Mrs Thorney, silver mounted Black Forest decanter; Mr J.N. Smith and Mr Brent Grotrian, silver mounted fantails; Mr C.A. Field, brass inkstand and candlesticks; Miss Cox Walker, china tea service; Mr and the Misses Little, silver egg stand; Master Stone, silver butter dish; Miss Hull, photo frame; Mr and Mrs Cromack, plush photo frame; Mr and the Misses Tause, hand-worked tea cosy; Miss Marshall, brush holder; Miss Bennet, picture; Mr Lynn, pictures; Mr Foster, box of sweetmeats; Mr and Mrs Bolton (Calcutta), Indian embroidery; Mrs Clarkson, tablecloths; Mrs Mabel Ayre, hand-painted white satin table centre; Mrs Hudson, shawls; Mrs K. Ellison, hand-worked tablecloths; Mr C.S. Bremmer, Indian embroidery. On a special table were the following: *Hull News* composing, commercial and literary staff, clock and bronzes; Scalby Cricket Club, silver salver; Scalby Choir, brass coal box; bride's Sunday school scholars, flower pot and stand; Scalby Day School, views of locality mounted in plush, and album; servants in The Hall, silver nut crackers and pinchers; servants at The Holt (which would include Mr and Mrs H. Kidd), brass inkstand; tenants of the bridegroom's father, flower tripod; Mr T. Tindall, flower vase and stand; Mrs Cockerill, hand-worked cushion; Widow's Alms Houses, toilet set; Mrs R. Boddy, glass jugs; Mr R. Boddy, wine glasses; Mr Thompson, brass inkstand; Mr T.W. and F. Thompson, ivory brush holder; Mrs Leadill, pin cushion; Mr Stephenson, Chippendale chair; Mr A. Cawton, copper letter rack; Mr and Mrs Bearecroft, oak bracket; Mrs Ward, newspaper rack; Miss Nelson, toilet mats; Miss Thompson, teacloths; Mrs Kent, hand-worked tablecloth; Mrs Jowsey, flower vases; Mrs T. Ralph, sardine box; Mrs Ralph, cheese dish; Miss Lightfoot, egg stand.

On the wedding of Mr J.A. Cooke's daughter, Miss Katherine Stephenson Cooke, to the Revd D'Arcy Strangways Morton, of Ripley, the villagers were, according to a newspaper report (dated by hand, 1 May 1890), no less enthusiastic in their admiration:

> The event created the most widespread interest . . . the school children [turned] out in full force with a profusion of primroses and other flowers to do honour to an esteemed resident of the village. On all sides colours and banners were displayed,

even the tower of St Lawrence's Church, where the ceremony took place, being adorned with flags. The interior of the church was beautifully decorated by the Misses Rudgard, Miss E. Biggs and others.

The church was crowded long before the hour fixed for the ceremony, and the arrival of the numerous guests was watched with the greatest interest by the spectators, many of whom had journeyed from Scarborough . . .

As the bridal party left the church, the approaches were strewn by the children with thousands of primroses and other flowers, while the organist played the 'Wedding March', and the bells rang out a merry peal. If it be true that 'happy is the bride that the sun shines on', then Mrs Morton is highly favoured, for as the happy couple drove away the sun shone out most brilliantly.

The presents were of the usual diversified character, costly and choice, several being of special interest. The employees of Mr Cooke, father of the bride, of the *Hull News*, sent a very handsome silver salver, the young men of the bride's bible class sent a choice framed photograph of the class, the village school children also sent a handsome present, while the members of the village reading-room presented a very pretty vase.

The guests were afterwards received at Scalby Holt by Mr and Mrs Cooke, the attendance being exceedingly numerous, the visitors including residents from all parts of the district.

The happy couple, Mr and Mrs Morton, left the village later in the day *en route* for Saltburn, where they spent their honeymoon . . .

It was further reported that the day after, 'the school children, choir, and others' were entertained to tea by Mr and Mrs Cooke in celebration of the event.

The Rudgard family of Scalby Hall had a second daughter, Olive Frances, who married, by coincidence, Henry John Rudgard, of Bootham, York, son of the then late John Rudgard, of Lincoln.

After the wedding, which was officiated over by the Revd R.W. Rudgard, brother of the bride, as well as the Revd W.C. Robinson, vicar of Scalby, it is reported that 'the wedding guests proceeded to Scalby Hall, where a reception was held, the Scarborough Rifle Volunteer Band playing a selection of music on the lawn, under the conductorship of Bandmaster J. Wall. The happy couple left by the 4.50 pm train for Wales, where the honeymoon [was] to be spent . . . '

No less impressive too was the list of presents, a number of which were given by members and tradesmen of the village.

Other weddings of note, lovingly remembered in the album of the Kidd family include that of the Hon. Rowland Tudor St John, Durham Light Infantry, third son of the late Lord and Lady St John of Bletsoe (Beds.) to Miss Katherine Madge Lockwood, youngest daughter of the late Sir Frank Lockwood, QC, MP, and of the late Lady Lockwood, of 26 Lennox Gardens, Chelsea.

It was given that, the 'wedding was kept as quiet as possible owing to the very recent death of the bride's mother, who had expressed a wish that the ceremony should not be postponed'.

The bride was given away by her uncle, Mr Alfred Lockwood, and Lord St John, of Bletsoe, acted as best man. Among the guests at the fashionable society wedding were the bridegroom's sisters, the Hon. Mrs Lawson Johnstone, Lady Lawrence, and the Hon. Anna Lawrence, Lady Swaythling, Lady Matthews, Mrs Alfred Lockwood, Lady Milman, Lady Jepson, Mrs Schwabe, Mrs Taylor, Mr and Mrs Kendal, Captain Mahon, Mrs Frank D'Arcy, Mrs James Jardine, and Mrs Godfrey Palmer. There was no reception afterwards, and it was quite early in the day when the bride left for Devonshire.

A newspaper report pasted opposite, of the will of Lady Lockwood, dated 10 Dec. 1908, records:

Dame Julia Rosetta Lockwood, of Raincliffe House, Scalby, Scarborough, and of 26 Lennox Gardens, London SW, formerly of Cober Hill, Cloughton, Scarborough, who died on the 16th September last, daughter of the late Mr Salis Schwabe, of Glyn-Garth, Anglesey, and of Manchester, and widow of Sir Frank Lockwood, QC, formerly Liberal MP for York, Recorder of Sheffield, and from 1894–5 Solicitor-General, left unsettled property of the gross value of £6,130 8s 4d, of which the net personalty was sworn at £5,619 5s 1d.

Lady Lockwood left her jewellery, household and personal effects, horses, carriages and consumable stores to her daughters, Lucy and Madge in equal shares. One hundred pounds was also left to her maid, Susan Tolman, if still in her service, or that of either of her daughters, at her decease.

Mention is also made of the Scalby weddings of the Hon. Violet Kitson, daughter of Lord Airedale, of Cober Hill, Cloughton, to Mr William G. Sheill; Captain Michael Graham (Tim) Thackray, of Horsforth, Leeds, to Miss Nancy Joan Elwiss, of Scalby, who was a member of the Staintondale Hunt, which formed an escort after the wedding in March 1946; and the York wedding of the daughter of the York Lady Mayoress, Miss Lydia Morrell, child of Mr J.B. Morrell and Mrs Morrell (Lady Mayor) to Mr A.H. Butler, which took place at the Friends' Meeting House, Clifford Street, York.

Theatricals played an important part in the entertainments of any community in the latter years of the nineteenth century and in the early years of this.

The Cook children, T. Percy and Katherine, his elder sister, both appeared in public in 'Amateur Theatricals' when, in January 1881, they played alongside each other in a 'juvenile company' at the Esplanade Gardens, Scarborough, in a production of *The Necklace*, an old-fashioned comedy in three scenes, which was followed in the second act, by the 'modern tragedy' of *Little Red Riding Hood*, an adaptation, with words by Tom Wood. The evening's entertainment was then concluded by a SALE OF WORK BY YOUNG FINGERS for the benefit of the Children's Hospital.

Others in the village were no less able in this field too. Miss Jean Rowntree told me how herself and others of the Rowntree family took part in the 'Scarborough Pageant' staged in the grounds of Peasholme Park; and I have made a mention earlier of the acting talents of 'Milly' Kidd in many school productions staged for the entertainment of Scalby villagers.

By contrast, death afforded no less an occasion for 'celebration' as marriage – though notably more sombre in character, and a village would turn out equally as enthusiastically to mourn the demise of a member of the 'gentry'.

Undoubtedly, it is possible that members of the Kidd family, and others of humble birth in Scalby, were present at the funeral of Lord Derwent on 4 March 1916. Certainly, the list of mourners records the presence of a substantial congregation from the village.

A lengthy newspaper account in the family album recalls:

From all parts of the town and countryside people flocked to pay their last tribute of respect to one who for so many years had been held in such high esteem by his neighbours. All shades of opinion and thought were represented round the graveside of the departed baron, and the attendance was remarkably representative of the many active and varied interests which Lord Derwent undertook in a well spent life.

Hackness, the home of the Johnstone family for the last 200 years, is one of the beauty spots of the Scarborough district. As a well-known writer described it: 'The scenery is such in hill and dale, plain and wood, moor and waterfall, continental in similitude, the traveller is reminded of some parts of Switzerland, whilst the comfortable homesteads of the tenantry scattered about give a peaceful and cheering addition to scenes of sylvan beauty'. Today the hand of winter was in evidence, but there were many indications of the approach of spring.

The picturesque old church at Hackness is named after St Hilda, and in the interior are fixed numerous memorials to the Johnstone family . . .

The remains of the late baron were interred in the family grave in the churchyard. The interior of the grave had been decorated with flowers and evergreens. The cortege left the Hall shortly before three o'clock and proceeded through the private grounds of the estate to the church. The coffin was conveyed from the Hall to the church on a bier, the bearers being drawn from tenantry on the estate. The body was enclosed in a shell or inner coffin. The outer coffin was of unpolished English oak, with brass Gothic fittings. At the top of the breastplate was placed a coronet, and the inscription was as follows:–

Harcourt,
Vanden-Bempde-Johnstone.
1st Baron Derwent.
Born 3rd January, 1829
Died 1st March, 1916.

The service was fully choral, and was conducted by the Rev. J.A. Pease (Vicar of Hackness) and the Rev. C. Johnstone, a relative of the deceased nobleman, and who for many years held the Vicariate of Hackness. . . . The last rites were performed amid a blaze of winter sunshine, which was almost immediately followed by a heavy downfall of snow and sleet.

The chief mourners were Captain, the Hon. Francis Johnstone; Sir Alan Johnstone, GVCO; the Hon. Louis Johnstone; the Hon. Gilbert Johnstone; Mrs Walter Long; Mr and Mrs H.W. St Quinton (Scampton Hall); Captain, the Hon. Ernest Willoughby; Colonel W.E. Duncombe; Miss Soans; Mr Edwin J. Pearce (private secretary to his Lordship); servants from the Hall and Estate.

Amongst those present in the church were: The Mayor of Scarborough (Mr C.C. Graham); Lord Londesborough; Brigadier-General Lord Basing, CB; Sir James Legard; Sir Everard and Lady Cayley; Captain, the Hon. Clive Behrens; Colonel Tilney; Major Hunter; Archdeacon Mackarness; the Rev. Cecil Cooper (Vicar of Scarborough); the Rev. F.G. Stapleton (Vicar of Seamer); the Rev. Arthur Hill (Thornton Dale); Dr Malvin (Scarborough); Dr Godfrey (Scarborough); Mr J. Dent, Mr A.F. Douglas (representing the Hon. Major Dawnay); Councillor T.H. Good (Scarborough); Mr Johnson Scott, Mr George Rowntree, JP, Mr W.S. Rowntree, JP, Mr H. Huggan, MFH (Scalby); Mr W. Hardcastle (Scalby); Mr R.S. Blaylock, Mr E. Barker (stationmaster, Scalby); Mr C. Leng (Scalby); Mr J. Little (Hackness); Mr J. Todd (Silpho); Mr E.H. Rudgard (Scalby); Mr A.H. Rudgard (Scalby); Mr W. Tingle Brown (Scalby); Mr Robert Hill (Thornton Dale); Mr E. Cockerill (Burniston); Mr G. White (Spikers Hill); Mr George Hill (Thornton Dale).

There were also present, representatives of the North Riding Magistrates; Scarborough Board of Guardians; the Royal Northern Sea Bathing Infirmary, including Mr Allan Rowntree; Scarborough Philosophical Society, which included Mr J.H. Rowntree; and a number of Freemason 'Brothers' were listed too.

At a lecture given in connection with the Scarborough Philosophical and Archaeological Society, held at the Museum . . . Mr S.P. Turnbull, the ex-president of the Society, moved that a vote of condolence should be sent to the relatives of the late Lord Derwent, who had been for many years president and patron of the Society. He mentioned the fact that the very stones of which the Museum was built came from the Hackness quarries, being the gift of the owner of the estate, who had taken the keenest interest in the institution from its earliest days. The word 'generous' was derived from the Latin 'generosus', meaning a man of noble birth, and Lord Derwent was distinguished by this quality. He had on one occasion offered a donation of £400 or £500 to the town for the institution of a public library, and it was a standing disgrace that the offer was not accepted. But Lord Derwent was not only generous in money, but was also generous in his appreciation of merit and ability wherever he came across it, and this kindly quality had endeared him to everyone who had had the honour of his acquaintance.

No doubt the funeral of Lord Airedale, of Gledhow Hall, and formerly of Cober Hill, Cloughton, was equally as impressive – certainly the legacy he left at the time was an estate of over one million pounds, made from his interests in steel in the West Riding town of Leeds. Among many bequests, he left money to employees at the Monkbridge Iron and Steel Company Ltd, and to Thomas Purvis Reay, of the Airedale Foundry, two of his companies.

His generosity was that he also left money to Leeds General Infirmary:

He further directed that the sum of £350,000 shall be invested in real estate and settled upon the uses of the Gledhow Estate, Leeds; and he bequeathed as heirlooms his portrait by Sargent, the mallet and trowel with which his father laid the foundation-stone of the Leeds General Infirmary, the casket and Freedom of the City of Leeds, which were presented to him, the Empire Gold Cup presented to him by his children on his 70th birthday, and the silver vase presented by Mrs Kitson and her children.

Lord Airedale had a passion for collecting old Leeds pottery, and it was said that the handsome wall cases at his home in Leeds contained one of the finest collections in the country – many acquired in Leeds, others bought at the sales in London.

Mention of Lord Airedale's portrait by J.S. Sargent reminds me that the artist painted another notable figure of the neighbourhood, Sir George and Lady Ida Sitwell and the children, which Sir George sent round the Scarborough electors. The Sitwell family, before their move to Wood End, at one time occupied Wrea Head, Scalby.

> The original picture was painted this spring [1900] by Mr Sargent, the most brilliant and famous of our living artists, and will appear in next year's Academy. It has been painted as a companion picture to an old group of the Sitwell family, executed in 1786 by Copley, and well known to many by Wood's beautiful mezzotint. . . . The group is admirably reproduced on the print sent out and long after the election[1] it will form in many a home an interesting souvenir of a memorable contest.

Familiar to many in Scalby still, will be the name of Halliday Huggan, of Crimbles Court. Miss Jean Rowntree thought him a great character. His obituary recounts that Mr Huggan

> was president of the Scarborough Cricket Club in 1945, and had been a member of the committee for over 21 years, and its representative on the committee of the Yorkshire County Cricket Club for nearly 12 years. He was honorary secretary of the Staintondale Hunt for 17 years, and its master from 1913 to 1921, and then, at the request of late Lord Derwent, he took over the honorary secretaryship of the Derwent Hunt, and also the management of the country, performing these duties for 21 years until he gave up riding two years before his death.

A Pudsey man, he came to live in Scalby in 1902, when on medical advice for a chest complaint it was suggested he live in the country.

> His long association with the Cricket Club dates from when, as a boy of seven or eight, he began to prefer going to the [Scarborough] ground to going to the sands.
>
> Once, during a holiday, he played for a Leeds club against Scarborough. From coming to the district in 1902 he played regularly for the Club for 20 years. He had attended practically every Scarborough Festival since 1886.
>
> He took up hunting only after coming to Scalby because of his fondness for horses and riding and the countryside, and few natives knew so well all the hedgerows and byways between Whitby and Hunmanby, or from the coast to Pickering and Lilla Cross. Cricket however, was his first love, and he always said that he valued the friendships which the game brought him more than the game itself. His interest in the Scarborough club and players never flagged, and one of the first telegrams of congratulations on attaining his Golden Wedding anniversary, which he celebrated just before his death, was from the president of Scarborough C.C., Sir Kenelm Cayley. After giving up playing he took up golf as a pleasant form of exercise rather than as a serious sport, and was a member of the North Cliff Golf Club.

The wedding of 'Kitty' Huggan, daughter of Mr Halliday Huggan, to Mr E.E. Goward, with the Staintondale
Hunt in attendance

Halliday Huggan served with the Artists Rifles, joining up in one of the later age
groups, during the war of 1914–1918, after having been a member of the local
volunteer force. He was a special constable at Scalby throughout World War II.

His family were woollen manufacturers, and his father, Thomas Huggan, was
joint founder with John Tunnicliffe's father, of the famous Pudsey Britannia Cricket
Club, of which Halliday Huggan was captain for some years.

He was survived in the village by his wife, a local Justice of the Peace and member of
the North Riding Bench for many years, to whom he was married in Silver Street
Methodist Church, Lincoln, by her father the Revd S. Walmsley. They had an only
daughter, Mrs E.E. Goward, who, with her husband, also well known in local cricket
circles, spent several years in India, before returning to live at the Farm Hotel, Woking, in
Surrey.

Talk of wills brings to mind that of Thomas E.J. Fenwick, of the Corner House, Scalby,
a partner in the firm of Martin & Fenwick, Civil Engineers and Surveyors, Park Row,
Leeds, who desired to be interred in the churchyard at Scalby. So afraid of being buried
alive, he directed that his trustees take all necessary steps to ensure that his death had
actually taken place before burying him, and to pay a medical man his fee for doing so.

Mr George Close, of West Mount Cottage, Church Becks, a retired joiner and builder
formerly of Sheffield, stated in his will:

I desire and express a fervent wish that each child of mine (Ida Victoria Close, West Mount Cottage; Helen Goodlad, 1 Beaconsfield Villas, and Harold Close, Home Farm, Scalby) participating in any way under this, my will – shall pay and contribute the annual sum of 5/- towards the maintenance and keeping in order, the graves of my mother, Betsy Close, and my late wife, Ellen Close, at Scalby . . .

Another notable figure in the village was Mr William Howgate, a churchwarden at St Lawrence's, and for some time, a manager of the local school. Married, the couple lived at Ravensdene, Scalby, firstly the home of his wife's father, Ephraim Fox, owner of Providence Mills, Staincliffe, in the West Riding. Mary, was the eldest daughter.

Mr and Mrs Howgate were married on 2 September 1857, at Dewsbury Parish Church, by the Revd Thomas Allbut. Both were born at Batley Carr, near Dewsbury, William, a third son, in a house overlooking the Church Schools, which was built by his father, James Howgate, a cloth manufacturer; while Mary, who was a sister of Major Chaley Fox, JP and Mrs Duke Fox, JP, first saw the light in a house situated a little distance away, near the then Co-operative Store.

Until leaving the Heavy Woollen District in 1898, Mr Howgate's life had been spent in the neighbourhood of Dewsbury. He resided for the greater portion of that time in Ravensthorpe, but for fourteen years he lived at Hopton.

William, in a newspaper interview published at the time of his Golden Wedding anniversary in 1907, recollected his early days spent at Batley Carr, where he first attended a 'Dame' school kept by Mrs Chadwick, afterwards serving as a pupil under Mr Joseph Wilby and Mr Samuel Illingworth. He recounted how on one occasion, a Shrove Tuesday, Mrs Thackrah, the mother of the then late Mr William Thackrah, assisted him and some other pupils, in locking out their schoolmaster so that they might have an 'extra' holiday.

Mr Howgate left school at fourteen, after being educated for a final year at St Knagg's School, Scarborough. This came about because his father travelled extensively in the Scarborough district, and had a stall in the market there for forty years where he sold his cloth. For some time after William had left school, business was carried out at Batley Carr under the title of Messrs James Howgate & Sons.

Later, they became partners in the Newtown Mill Company (Albion Mill) at Ravensthorpe – 'Newtown' being at that time, the name of the district. In 1860 they commenced the erection of Ravensthorpe Mills. From the very commencement of its growth Mr Howgate recalled how he identified himself 'heart and soul' with Ravensthorpe. 'Ravensthorpe', he declared, 'was purely the outcome of Batley Carr manufacturers transferring their businesses there. And it was a beautiful district in those days.' Mills were built there by the following firms in the order written: Day Nephew & Son, Fox & Pickles, Edward Hemingway (Brooklyn Mills), Walker Bros., and Messrs James Howgate & Sons. 'Our engine was started', he continued, 'on the anniversary of my wedding in 1861. We had the severest winter on record during the years 1860–1. There was a frost which lasted thirteen weeks and the masons never lifted a shovel nor touched a stone during the whole of that time. It commenced a few days before Christmas and lasted into March. The Calder [river] was actually frozen over, and people could go over with carts.'

William Howgate was, for a period, president of the Manufacturers' Association, formed about 1874, for the purpose of fixing wages and arranging other matters concerning the local industry. He was also a trustee of the Dewsbury Infirmary for most of his life, having held that office since the institution was built. It is said that both Mr and Mrs Howgate always took a deep interest in the infirmary and many other charitable works. Mrs Howgate was a tireless worker among the sick and poor of the district, and served as president of the Ladies Committee of the Dewsbury Infirmary; she also served in a similar capacity in connection with the Mirfield Cottage Hospital.

At the funeral of Mrs Mary Howgate, who departed this earth before her husband on 12 May 1913, aged seventy-nine, family were still living at Scalby including Masters G.H. and C.E. Fox, great nephews. Others of the village who attended included Miss Hannah Pearson, a maid who had been at Ravensdene seven years, Mrs E. Kidd, and a number of the schoolchildren, under the charge of the schoolmaster, Mr J. Tickle, who were present at the funeral in recognition of the interest Mrs Howgate took in the running of the school.

It is recorded that the grave was lined with evergreens, forget-me-nots, geraniums, violas and narcissi, by the sexton, Mr G.L. Bastiman.

Later 'sons' of Scarborough who resided in Scalby, and perhaps deserve a mention here, must be Tom and Frank Laughton, brothers of the cinema star, Charles Laughton, who himself, and his wife, Elsa Lanchester, when in England, lived at Levisham, off the main Whitby–Pickering road. The mother of Lord Baden-Powell often took up summer residence at Levisham Hall.

The Laughton family lived at Scarborough, and are still remembered by a plaque affixed to the hotel of their birth opposite the railway station. Frank Laughton came to Scalby in 1955 from the Pavilion, and left in 1963 when he sold his house in the village and moved to a flat in London.[2]

His brother Tom, a notable hotelier in the district, published his autobiography in 1977. In it, he recalls his later life at Scalby with his second wife, Esmé Holliday, and how their home played an important role in providing for his 'business'.

> In the spring of 1944 I met Esmé Holliday, a beautiful young woman from Scarborough who was serving as an officer in the WRNS. We had known each other at home, but in a period when I was wasting my time philandering. She was tall, with chestnut hair, grey-blue eyes, a lovely skin, fine features and a striking high-spirited carriage. She looked stunning in her naval uniform. She was stationed in London quarters close to Hyde Park. We saw a great deal of each other, I fell in love with her, and eventually persuaded her to marry me as soon as I became free.
>
> I had married my first wife outside the Catholic Church; this time I wanted to be married with the blessing of the Church. . . .
>
> As soon as my divorce became absolute, Esmé and I were married in the Catholic church of St James, Spanish Place, London, in January 1945. Our marriage had a disastrous start. Only three days after the wedding, during a brief honeymoon in Brighton, the news came that Esmé was in desperate trouble. I will not record in detail what was involved, but the outcome was public disgrace and our being separated for nearly a year . . .
>
> I bought a beautiful house standing on eight acres of good land at Scalby, three miles outside Scarborough, and when Esmé and I returned to Yorkshire we set up home there. When we returned . . . everyone went out of their way to make us welcome. We received a round of invitations, some from people that we scarcely knew. It was a heartening experience.

The hotel [Royal Hotel, Scarborough] was in a shocking condition after six years of war. I took Esmé to see it and when she saw the condition at the front of the house and behind, she blanched. For the first year she was so busy setting up our home that she rarely visited the hotel. It was busy enough but the standards were dreadful and it was a relief to close it down at the end of the season.

During the winter we explored the hotel together. Esmé had been brought up in the hotel business. She realised immediately the magnitude of the task that lay in front of us. 'We can't get this right living at Scalby', she said, 'we shall have to live in the hotel'. So, by the time it re-opened in the following spring, we had moved in.

Esmé's capability was a revelation. She quickly gathered together an effective housekeeping staff, and although the hotel was in a shabby and badly equipped condition, she soon made it sparkle. Our new home in Scalby had a good garden and with it we had inherited an experienced gardener [Raymond Hopkins]. All the flowers were sent in to the hotel, where they compensated to a certain degree for the drab surroundings. The garden was to become one of the principal features of the hotel, as it enabled us to make lavish use of flowers. It was developed with the needs of the hotel in mind; hot-house plants to fill the jardinière that was a feature of the entrance hall; flowers specially grown to fill the urn that stood facing the hotel entrance; even Christmas roses for the Christmas season. Mrs Haddon, the hotel florist, became one of the most important members of the staff, working hand in glove with Raymond, the gardener at Scalby . . .

We came home to Scalby in October, 1964.

At home, we settled down to retirement. It distressed Esmé to walk up the stairs, so we decided to build bedrooms on the ground floor, so that we would be able live on one level. We came to the decision in 1965 but it was the spring of 1966 before the work was put in hand, and then it took approximately a year to complete. I had another building project in view. For many years I had longed to have a walled garden. I had even considered moving house to get one, but we were too attached to our home. So the only way was to build a wall around our existing kitchen garden. It was sheltered from the east and sloping gently down to the south. I decided to build a wall on the north and west sides, one hundred and ten yards long and twelve feet high. It took us a year during which time we laid forty-one thousand bricks! I built it together with John Wardle, the husband of our cook. John took the leading part. It leans a little in places, but it is a grand wall and has proved a great asset to the garden.

Whilst we were building the wall, Raymond Hopkins, our gardener, made his third attempt to establish an asparagus bed. As we had had two failures, I made a study of asparagus culture and wrote a thesis on it. Raymond made the bed on the lines laid down in my thesis. This time, he was successful and we now have a well established bed, which provides one of the highlights of the gardening year. It is one of my most prized possessions.[3]

Finally, we cannot leave a chapter on the 'personages' of Scalby without a mention of a family that helped to shape the district in no uncertain terms, and in other ways, played a small part in the compilation of this work, albeit in an unbeknown role – the Rowntree family – in particular, Mr John W. Rowntree and later his widow, Mrs Constance

Langdale End from Broka – Langdale was the later home of the Rowntree family after leaving Scalby

Margaret Rowntree, who died on 9 March 1928, leaving in her will among many bequests, the sum of £200 each to Reginald Minshall and Jane Ann Vernon in acknowledgement of their long and faithful service; £50 each to her servants Ethel Nixon and Ernest R. Minshall; and the sum of £10 to her servant John Lawrence Minshall.

Probate of her will was granted to her daughters, Miss Jean Wilhelma Rowntree of Langdale End, Hackness, Mrs Margaret Rowntree Crossley, of Barfield, Brandsby, and Mrs Sarah Antoinette Baldwin, of 95 High Street, Harrow, Middlesex, and her brother-in-law, Benjamin Seebohm Rowntree, manufacturer, of The Homestead, York.

Following is a brief portrait of John Wilhelm Rowntree, taken from an extensive introductory sketch found in the book, *John Wilhelm Rowntree: Essays and Addresses*, edited by Joshua Rowntree (published by Headley Brothers, London, second edition, 1906, for the Friends' Book Centre), which is well worth a study for its insight into the Quaker movement.

It is understood that in the first half of the 18th century, when the parental home was a farmhouse still to be seen a mile or so north of Hutton Rudby, in Cleveland, one William Rowntree was sent adrift portionless because he had turned Quaker. He afterwards married, took the Riseborough farm, near Pickering, and brought up his family there. His son John migrated to Scarborough, founded a grocery business, and married Elizabeth Lotherington, who added sweetness to his strength. Their third son, Joseph, moved to York, established there a similar business, and married Sarah Stephenson, who combined saintliness with excellent judgement: he became a leading member of the City Council, of Committees of the Friends' Schools and Retreat, and of many other philanthropic bodies, and was largely instrumental in abolishing the suicidal custom of disownment for 'marrying out' in the Society of Friends.

Their second son, Joseph, who married as his second wife E. Antoinette Seebohm, became the head of the cocoa firm, and is widely known as the co-author of *The Temperance Problem*. The Seebohms are said to be descended from an officer in the Swedish army, who went over to Germany with Gustavus Adolphus during the Thirty Years' War and afterwards settled in that country.

John Wilhelm, born on the 4th September, 1868, was the eldest son of this marriage. He grew up in the city of York, in a home in which hospitality and thought for others were portions of his inheritance. It was enlivened as the years went on by a family of four brothers and two sisters. One who knew him well writes:–

'As a child, although very affectionate, he was of a passionate nature, and he had to struggle against this weakness certainly well into his school life. He had a highly nervous temperament. He was always truthful and honourable, but had to fight against selfishness. He was a very close observer, was always imaginative, a great mimic, and fond of acting. He had a German nurse, and spoke German before he could speak English. His deafness interfered with the enjoyment of his school life, and probably was then acutely felt. A power of composition was early shown in childish harangues to his companions, and in essays contributed to the School Essay Society. He had the artistic temperament strongly developed, with a great sense of beauty in nature and art. He showed considerable facility in fine pen and ink work, and occasionally did a little oil painting, but made little use of these gifts, except for diagrams and illustrations for his Adult School lessons.'

John was educated at the Friends' School at Bootham, with an intermediate tarriance at Oliver's Mount School at Scarborough. He was not distinguished in his classes, caring more for men than mathematics, and the deafness already alluded to shut him out from many of the games of the playground. To the onlooker he would have passed as a delicate child, observant and quick, not sympathetic, inclined to be quizzical, and for a schoolboy, careful of his appearance.

One master in describing his final year at Bootham, writes:

'His difficulty in hearing had already begun to show itself. He always sat by me to be able to hear, and when I had occasion to use the blackboard he followed me there. I always felt that he was a most appreciative pupil, anxious to learn and to miss nothing, and very grateful for any little one could do in helping him to take full advantage of his last year of school life'.

On leaving school he went at once into the Cocoa works at York, and though not naturally methodical, he applied himself to business with extraordinary energy and diligence. Beginning in a very subordinate position, he rapidly fitted himself for more responsible posts, and won and retained the esteem and friendship of the employees with whom he was associated.

With a restless and inquisitive mind which familiarised itself with many departments of knowledge, and was determined when possible to test things for itself, it was inevitable that the waves of modern doubt should break heavily upon him. For a few years he experienced great religious unsettlement. . . . Whilst he was still struggling to obtain a secure foundation foothold of faith, religion came to John Wilhelm Rowntree the most real quest of his life. Humanity stood out before him as the highest of created things, and yet as sorely in need of compassion and of uplifting. He recognised the many ways in which sympathy could be shown, and aid be given to man, in body, soul, and spirit. He was keenly interested in art, in politics, in social reform, and in education, but religion to him held the key of all the rest; and as it grew to be a living reality in his own experience, he spared no time or thought or trouble to make it a reality to others.

His eagerness for a more spiritual life in himself, and for more of its liberty and power in the meetings of the Society to which he belonged, found vent in 1893 in a pamphlet entitled, *A few thoughts upon the position of young Friends in relation to the Society.*

This pamphlet brought in a vast correspondence to its author. Though ready with his pen, he was not a great letter writer. One of his letters in 1897 begins, 'Probably I am the worst letter writer in England', but this is hardly an impartial statement.

Indeed, this fact was undoubtedly untrue, for up until his death, J.W. Rowntree engaged in many varied correspondences. He wrote often to the editor of *The Friend* magazine on Quaker matters, and such an example of the diversity of those matters is repeated below in a published letter pasted into the Kidd album:

To the Editor of The Friend

DEAR FRIEND,– The following, extracted from the parish register of Hackness under the date 1653, may be of interest to readers of THE FRIEND.

1653,

Richard Cockerell dyed on Wednesday, the XIII. day of September, and was buryed the next day, being Thursday. And there was many of them they call Quakers at his buryell. And Mr Prowde did exhorte and argue with them at the grave, and they held out that that worke wch they had in them was not wrought by the worde, wch I was sorry to heare; but they sayd they made use of the word only to try whether it were right or noe. (Hackness Parish Register)

I believe the first mention of the word 'Quakers' in the records of Parliament was in 1654. It is interesting to notice that the word coined at Derby in 1650 by Mr Justice Bennet should so soon have found its way into the register of a parish on the north-east coast of Yorkshire.– I am, your friend sincerely,

J. Wilhelm Rowntree.

Silverdale, Scalby, R.S.O., Yorks,
    20th April, 1903.

In early life, one important factor in the growth of John's thought and character, was Adult School work, which had long been carried on in York.

On leaving school, he accompanied his father for some time to the parent Adult School in Lady Peckett's Yard, but after a few years the determination to launch out into extension work grew upon him, and, almost single-handed, he established a school in the neighbouring village of Acomb. A number of railway employees had come to live in the village, and the eager young teacher soon gathered a large company of intelligent men around him. Many of them were largely imbued with the questioning spirit of the age, and no commonplace presentations of truth would suffice to hold them. John rose early and sat up late to prepare his Sunday lessons. Piles of note books and MSS. remain to show the pains he took to give his hearers the best within his reach. The most varied fields of knowledge were searched for their spoils, and the reapings were all made to subserve the deepest purpose in life . . . [an] ex-scholar has since written of his former teacher, 'He was one who could lead, for he evinced the wisdom we could trust. We have all too few of such teachers . . . Our good men are frightened at the depths, so keep in shallow water which is not buoyant'.

The development of the firm's estates led to more than one visit to the West Indies. He travelled also in Mexico, Egypt, and Syria, in addition to his many journeys to the United States. The diaries which remain of some of these tours are very readable and racy.

On 28th July, 1892, John Wilhelm Rowntree was married to Constance M. Naish, of Bristol. His home life, first at York and then at Scalby, was one of exceeding happiness. It was lavishly shared with friends of all ranks and conditions. Though his wife ever relieved him of household cares, he did not lose sight of home duties in the far vistas that were constantly opening out before him . . .

Allusion has been made to his early deafness. As the years went on a serious contraction of power of sight, greatly restricting his vision, took place. In any dim light he could no longer see the way before him. The stumbling over a child on one occasion pained him much. One of the best physicians was consulted. He could hold out no hope of improvement, or even of the arrestment of the evil . . .

A paragraph in a letter written shortly afterwards to Lawrence Richardson, one of his most intimate friends, is characterstic in its prompt acceptance of the situation in which he found himself, and in his determination to make the best of it.

'October 17th, 1894.

'My complaint is Retinitis pigmentosa, and Nettleship and Hutchinson have given me up. While writing, I may as well inform you that I have at last finally undertaken the pamphlet campaign. W.C.B. Grubb, Agnes Smithson and myself are a sort of committee, and I am to receive the papers and print and distribute them. We think of calling them Present Day Papers, and numbering them, printing in rich old black type on rough paper, ragged edges, with thorough artistic get-up, and arrange for one person in each big Quaker centre to act as distributor. They are to be perfectly straight, and to have the definite aim of waking up the Society to thought'.

The occasional papers here anticipated grew in time into a monthly periodical, which lasted for several years. The volumes (from 1899 to 1902) are full of thoughtful articles and informing reviews.

Though perforce an ambassador in bonds, he was yet no invalid. He had great enjoyment in life, and remained strong physically. His abounding labours put the inertia of most men without any such limitations to shame. He put himself under an American specialist, and for a time, at the cost of severe regimen and treatment, the onward ravages of the complaint were stayed . . .

In 1889 John was ordered to give up town life and daily attendance at business, and betake himself to a country home. He chose a house at Scalby, near Scarborough, quickly found pleasure in his new surroundings, gave himself eagerly to his garden, and began, as he said to 'intensify cabbages'. Happily this application

The drawing-room of 'Friedensthal' was decorated and furnished for many years in almost pure 'Art Nouveau' style from the furniture, including the elegant writing desk in the corner, and the basket chair, to the wallpaper

of chemistry reacted favourably on himself, and injured nobody. In reality the change of residence enabled him to give much of the energy hitherto devoted to business to objects nearer his heart. He turned with redoubled desire to the 'intensifying' of the Society of Friends.

In person, John Wilhelm Rowntree was tall and erect, his figure gained in breadth and strength during his country life. He had a frank and manly bearing; and in later years especially, there was always the readiness for a smile behind his straightforward earnestness of purpose. Both in appearance, and often in the opening words of an address, there were reminders of his Teuton ancestry. The depicting of him as 'with blind eyes luminous' is not inapt. Any one watching him felt that the gates that barred his vision only shut out the foreground, not the distance . . .

Some of his later activities included the 'Guest House' at Scalby. John used to say that the danger of a comfortable country home was the lessening of opportunity for serving others. One of the objects of the Guest House was to safeguard his children from such a snare. The Executive Committee of the Yorkshire Adult Schools had already tried the experiment of establishing a holiday home for their members, but the results had not justified its continuance. John's offer of 'Friedensthal' ('The Valley of Peace') – a detached house with spacious grounds at Scalby, on generous terms, induced the hope that a second attempt might prove more permanent, and after conference between the Lessor and Lessees, the undertaking was launched on a wider basis than before. As the scheme matured John was building a home for himself on land adjoining the Guest House [this was Low Hall]. He needed and deserved a quiet home more than most men, but he

'Friedensthal', which means 'Valley of Peace', opened as an Adult School Guest House in 1904. It was rented from J.W. Rowntree of Low Hall and ran until about 1920. Later it became Uplands School for private pupils, and was eventually demolished. It was situated about where the entrance to Wordsworth Close is now, on the Hackness Road. The district was noted for its Adult Schools, organized by the Society of Friends (Quakers), and holidays at these places were the 'in thing' for many years. When 'Friedensthal' closed, Cober Hill, at Cloughton took on the role of Adult School Guest House

planned it for others as much as himself. The hall was to be large enough for lectures, and on the second floor was a long and pleasant dormitory with fifteen cubicles, to take in an overflow of guests from 'Friedensthal' on occasions of pressure. The erection of a pavilion was also contemplated, for the accommodation of week-end conferences, or local Summer Schools . . .

The winter of 1904–5 was one of abounding effort and far-reaching thought. The sudden death of his brother-in-law, Ernest Grace of Bristol, which came very closely home to him, sent him on his way with ever renewed faith and diligence. The winter before, John Wilhelm had laid down the lines of a history of Quakerism, – a modern Apologia for its place in Christendom. He estimated that it would prove a ten years' task. 'I shall hope', he wrote, 'so to proportion my work day by day, – as to keep the study going, and at the same time remain sufficiently in touch with contemporary affairs, although undoubtably this undertaking involves a certain withdrawal from work which would otherwise have been undertaken'.

Upwards of two thousand volumes and pamphlets collected together for this work prove the hold it had taken upon him. In addition he had prepared the materials for six lectures on the Christian's faith as verified in his own experiences, and these he had hoped to give in various centres. The building of his own home, and the starting of the Guest House, have been referred to. He was hoping to take part in a general Summer School at Sidcot, and to undertake the secretarial work, and to prepare some historical lectures for a social school at Scalby, planned by his Monthly Meeting at his own request for the ensuing summer. Largely at his instance, it had been arranged to hold a week-end Yorkshire Quarterly Meeting at Scarborough in the spring [1905], with two sittings devoted to a Conference on the subject of the Ministry; and further, he was throwing himself with keen interest into plans for making the holding of the Yearly Meeting at Leeds the occasion for a forward movement in the Society of Friends throughout the north of England, as he firmly held it ought to be.

The holding of the Yearly Meeting in the provinces, after some two and a quarter centuries of London Yearly Meetings only, was in itself largely due to his advocacy, and to his strong desire that this annual gathering should tell more upon the life of the world around it. Early in the present year [1905], in the midst of all these hopes and efforts, John's sight was again a cause of anxiety, and a visit to his American specialist loomed suddenly before him. The treatment on the last occasion had been painful, but he never hesitated. For himself, he said he would prefer to stay at his work and take the risks; but his powers were a trust for others, and so the best advice obtainable must decide. He chose to go at once, in order that he might be back before the Yearly Meeting.

Shortly before sailing, he presided at the annual meeting of shareholders of the firm in which he was a director, making a masterly speech on the aims and policy of the business, and the importance of the social work carried on among the employees. His last Sunday in England was spent at York. He gave an address in connection with the laying of the foundation stone of a new Adult School at Burton Lane . . .

The front of Low Hall, Scalby, now owned by the National Union of Mineworkers, and used as a convalescent home

His wife accompanied him to America, intending to return in time for the opening of the Guest House. On the voyage John was seized with a severe attack of pneumonia. Dr Rufus Jones [editor, *American Friend*] happily met the vessel on its arrival, and the unconscious invalid was conveyed to the New York Hospital, where he received every possible attention. There was no recovery, only a quieting down of the fever. He died on the 9th March 1905.

John Wilhem Rowntree never saw the opening of his 'Guest House' – Low Hall – but his good works went on. Nor did he witness the wedding of his daughter Antoinette to Mr R.M. Baldwin on 20 August 1925, at St Mary's Church, Hackness. However, a blessing was that he was spared the death of his son, killed in action during the First World War – but Henry Kidd and his family, including his daughter 'Milly', felt them all, and were present at most. Ironically, Henry was, by the time he came into the employ of Mrs J.W. Rowntree, suffering from partial deafness, which also had an affect on his balance. By this period, the widow had moved into Low Hall from Silverdale, their first residence in Scalby, and Mr and Mrs Kidd remained in service with Mrs Rowntree for over twenty years until his retirement, at which time, he and his wife, who had cooked for the Rowntree family, continued to lovingly compile their 'family' history.

NOTES

1. The election was in 1900 between Sir George Sitwell (Con) and Sir Compton Rickett (Lib) who won. Sir George died in 1903.
2. Laughton, Tom, *Pavilions by the Sea: Memoirs of a Hotel-Keeper*, Chatto & Windus, London, 1977.
3. Ibid.

CHAPTER EIGHT

Full Steam Ahead

The area around Scalby is well-watered, streams abound, one rising 'on the approach to the eastern entrance of Scalby . . . a fine spring of chalybeate water which deposits its ochry and russet dye on the adjacent channel'.[1] This was often referred to as the *Spaw*, although in no sense did it enjoy the reputation which many in the neighbourhood enjoyed. In fact the village considered it somewhat of a nuisance, as it caused a perpetual muddy mess on the thoroughfare; so it was put underground, and now drains into the 'Cut' just below Newby Bridge.

Undoubtedly the water-table of the district was fed by an abundance of rain, although Cole describes 'the climate of Scalby [is] very favourable, the air being singularly pure and salubrious; but the west-winds, sweeping from the moor, are most piercing and detrimental during their prevalence'.[2]

Severe storms were more common in those times. A number are mentioned. In September 1823, Anne Lister, of Shibden Hall, Halifax, while on holiday in Scarborough, wrote in her diary:

The Old Mill, Scalby

Sunday 14th

In the evening, from 6.45 to 8, M– & Lou & little Charles Milne & I sauntered along the North sands as far as Scorby [Scalby] Mill. Darkish when we got back. . . . Perhaps about 12½ [at night], every door & window in the house seemed to rattle, which disturbed us exceedingly. At 1st, we thought someone [was] breaking into the house but the continuance of the noise & the pattering of rain soon ushered in a tremendous thunder storm. Very vivid, fast-succeeding flashes of lightning enlightened the whole room. After some time came 1 or 2 tremendous peals of thunder & the heaviest rain I almost ever heard.[3]

In August 1857:

A great storm did much damage at Scalby. The house of a poor man was swept away, the family escaping with their lives almost miraculously. A great many houses were flooded to the depths of five or six feet, and some of them very much injured. One poor man had a small haystack and part of his garden washed away by the devastating element; the neighbouring mills very much damaged; both the bridges near the Church were washed away; and the hedges in many places were torn up by the roots. The sands, after the storm, from Scalby mill tea gardens to Peasholme presented a sad scene – the immense quantity of *debris* including trees, broken bridges, dead pigs, &c., brought down by the flood. Much damage was done to the crops.[4]

At one time all water for household use was obtained from wells, pumps or springs. Apart from private wells in yards or houses, there were several public ones, marked on the Ordnance Survey maps as 'well' or 'D well', which were for common use. These appear most frequent in the North Street area.

There is little evidence of these today, but one of the old-fashioned pumps in its wooden case stands against the north wall of Home Farm; and not far away is an all-metal type at the back of Scalby Hall. Most of the wells have been filled in or covered over. A very fine example was discovered by accident at Gate House in the late 1950s. It is about 20 ft deep and 4 ft in diameter, and the dry brick-work is intact.

Elsewhere, the valley of the River Derwent provided the main supply of water for the district. The original course of the river became blocked by ice and boulder clay during the Ice Age, which ended some 10,000 years ago, and a new course cut itself through, forming what is known today as 'Forge Valley', before entering the sea at Scalby Mills. Unfortunately the amount of flooding for long periods that ensued over large areas of agricultural land, meant that drainage was essential, if settlement and full farming potential was to be attained. Consequently, towards the end of the eighteenth century, following disastrous flooding in 1799, it was suggested that a branch of the River Derwent be formed into a canal to cut through the hump of land holding it back, only a few feet above the level of the river, and so drain the area.

Cole records:

The 'Report, published in 1800, by William Chapman, Esq., Engineer, on the means of draining the low grounds in the vales of the Derwent and Hertford' recommended the formation of this canal, in the following words:

Scalby Mills: an engraving published by T. Taylor & Son, from a painting by Hornibrook, dated 1897

'On quitting the mountains the Derwent passes through a narrow defile, immediately above which there is a broad gap in the ridge toward the sea; through which opening nothing prevents the river from flowing but an extended plain gently rising for upward of a mile, and then declining to the ocean. This flat ground is nearly half a mile in width between the hills, and in its summit only rises, according to the best information I could acquire, about eighteen inches above the highest floods in the river; which in this part do not exceed ten feet perpendicular height. The summit is a moory earth for about four feet in depth, and sand for some feet below it. The fall from thence to the road from Hackness to Scarborough, and onward to the Scalby road, appears to be moderate; and to within less than half a mile of the Whitby road seems not to be so steep as to make the water ungovernable that might be brought through this pass; thenceforward it becomes steeper, and the vale narrower, so that the rivulet running through it, has, by its meandering torn down the brows of the high ground into precipices, and has, in fact, been more destructive than a river, whose reflection, if even left to itself, would not be so frequent. The proposed course of the river would pass the mills above the Whitby road. Below is a mill in disuse, and one in good repair close to the sea, near to which the vale on both sides is bounded by rocks'.[5]

The Muston & Yeddingham Drainage Co., later merged with the Ouse Catchment Board, was formed to carry out the project. William Chapman was appointed the engineer. There was more to it however, than just cutting away a few feet of earth. For one thing bridges had to be built at Everley, and where two roads crossed the river in Scalby.

Scalby Sea Cut: Upper Scalby Bridge over the watercourse, one of three bridges between here and the sea

One of the two bridges was Newby Bridge, on the Burniston coastal road, below the incline leading to Scalby Manor Hotel. Before 1800 there was a ford at that point for wheeled traffic. The river – hardly more than a stream – was so small that a footbridge served pedestrians, built, it is said, of one large stone flag.

When the first bridge was erected at the time of building the 'Cut', as the canal (opened in 1804) became known, the villagers could not bear to see this fine stone wasted, so it was transferred to Foulsyke to span the little stream that runs across the road there. It still exists, but the stream was later diverted a foot or two through a bricked arch.

In 1906 Newby Bridge was rebuilt and widened so as to include a footpath on one side. The cost was about £900. Unfortunately, to save expense, this bridge was not made in line with the approaches, but formed an S-bend. So for the sake of safety, it had to be demolished to be replaced by the present structure.

The last function of the Court Leet was connected with the waterways. This was the biennial 'beck-viewing'. A bailiff collected his jury and they trudged along the banks of the waterways, looking out for obstructions, etc. They presumably had power to 'fine' transgressors! After a hard day the party then retired to one of the inns for dinner. This 'beck-viewing' died out shortly after the First World War.

In the nineteenth century, a private company was formed to provide the village with piped water. A good supply was found beyond Keld Runnels farm [Scalby Nabs], and was lifted into a reservoir at East Nabs by an automatic hydraulic ram. Later this responsibility was taken over by the then Scalby Urban District Council, and proved satisfactory till the increase in the number of houses after 1918 made a further supply essential.

After many tests, a boring 180 ft deep was made in the flat land to the south of Scalby Nabs in 1940. Two new reservoirs, capable of holding 200,000 gallons, were then constructed at some 500 ft above sea-level and water was pumped into them for the use of the district.

With the drainage of the neighbourhood came an increased and better road system between Scalby and Scarborough, and northward to Whitby, and inland to Hackness, where a 'new road' was constructed around 1800 by 'Sir Richard Vanden Bempde Johnstone, Bart., the proprietor of Hackness, at about £600 of his own expense'.[6]

Horses, of course, took the most significant role before the advent of the motor car. Of private vehicles there were many types, from the modest little governess-cart, with seats running fore and aft, to the sophisticated sprung landau of the wealthy. In between the two came the gig, a compact vehicle much favoured by farmers; and the horse-drawn vehicle had one great advantage over its petrol rival at a time when both travelled the highways and byways together – it could always find its own way home unaided, particularly when a farmer had had a drop too much ale on market day!

When the motor car first appeared in Scalby, few believed in the decline of the horse as a motive power. Most forms of transport relied on the horse for pulling – farm wagons, carriers, 'carriage' trade, even ploughing – and such as Henry Kidd and his son, and many like them, coachmen, grooms and so on, felt secure in their employment. The motor car was a 'fad', a passing phase, an attitude best illustrated in a 'fictional' story cut out from a newspaper and pasted into the family album as an admonitory lesson on the 'feckleness' of this new invention – although it is perhaps fair to say that the coming of the 'horseless-

Jockey carriage *c.* 1895. A popular mode of transport in which to ride out from Scarborough and view the delights of Scalby. Each carriage was in the charge of a 'professional' jockey, in this case the rider, Hopkins

carriage' did not create such a state of surprise as one might have expected when Mr J.A. Cooke introduced the first into Scalby in the 1890s. After all, the bodywork was done by the coach-builder, and the early cars were very much like the dog-cart. It is said greater excitement was aroused hereabouts when a lady cycled through the village clad in bloomers!

Nevertheless, the general opinion is well exemplified in the story below:

PA'S MOTOR-CAR.

MY DEAREST OWN ETHEL,– I have been such a *miserable* girl since I saw you. I have even been reading 'Milton', dear, and other serious works, I have been *so unhappy.*

For I didn't win that tennis racquet at our contest; Eva Bell won it; because I didn't get to the ground *at all* that day; because pa *would* take me in his *absurd* motor-car. I shall *cry* in a minute – and Eva Bell said she was *so* sorry I couldn't come. *Thing*!

I told pa I'd better not go in the car, because it was so *important* I should *get there*; but he *would* take me. We started nicely, after a while; at least, I mean the car didn't run backwards into the garden whistling, as it sometimes will, and try to climb the front steps up to ma!

When we got to the foot of the hill, pa was able to look round for a moment, and he smiled. (He's such a *dear* old dad, but so *absurd*.) 'Bounces, don't it?' he said; he's so *proud* of that car; and then he saw the garden gate trailing after us in the road. Because he had forgot to untie the car when he started!

And he *left* me there, and carried it back. Only *think! alone* in that frightful car by myself. I wonder I never *screamed*. It was all trembling and bubbling horribly, *somewhere* – inside! You've no *idea*! And it *quarrels to itself*, and I thought it might go off, or take fright; at least, not take fright, but run away, same thing – *fancy*! And I was *so* thankful when dad came back. He brought our old brown horse with him, and tied it on behind. To give 'Prince' some *exercise*, he said; but I *know* it was because he has had to come back for him *lots of times* to drag that ridiculous car home.

If I was a horse I'd be *indignant* to dangle behind a *motor-car* that way – so idiotic! And perhaps old 'Prince' *was*; because he *would* walk sideways, and he took up all the road, and carts couldn't get by, and were *so* rude to pa, and boys came long distances, dear, quite *tired* with running, to say insulting things about the car, which *stopped*, and the old horse, which *smiled – fancy*!

They called it 'Old Fork Lightning' – *cheek* – and asked us 'was it drove by *electricity*?' and 'was this its *funeral* trip?' and *lots* else. And we couldn't go away; till, at last, the car jerked so funny, and fizzed, and went on – *suddenly*. And pa smiled again, and said 'he *knew* it would go – sometime or other – if we only *waited*!'

But those boys (how *horrid* boys are – so are *men*; at least, some *men*, I mean) those boys had untied the horse, and pa never knew, and drove the car that *slowly*, because of 'Prince's' old age and knees; and I *knew* I'd be *late*! I just *knew*, dear!

And at Brashery Corner, *of course*, the car wouldn't turn round the *right way*, and pa *pretended* it was much *prettier scenery* round Detchwater way; only *think*! and it's a whole *lots* further!

And he never knew till we got to Detchwater Bridge that the old horse wasn't behind us, and then he *left* me again, and went to look for it – quite *worried* now.

Oh! and a grocer's young man asked me, dear, would I 'move the car a trifle, miss,' so that he could 'drive past, miss'; and, of course, I *dared* not touch the levers, and some men pushed the car to the side of the road, and it seemed to *wake up*, somehow, and began to work *of itself*! And it shook like a jelly, and began to rattle down into the *river*, and it stood there, coughing, dear, and scratching up the mud and water with its *hind legs* – at least, its back wheels, I mean, same thing – like a *dog! Fancy*!

Just only *think*, dear! It splashed all over me, and quite ruined *everything*, and it was the hat I gave so *much* for, and you'd never seen it – with pinks bows – only I wrote to you that long letter about it. *You* remember, don't you?

And the wheels *wouldn't* stop, and they wouldn't try to make them, on *purpose*, I feel sure; because they laughed so much – coarse, unsympathising laughs – and a dog that *barked*!

And then pa came back, so *upset*, and they hitched the old horse on, and that *idiotic* car suddenly tried to climb over its back, and the machinery unexpectedly burst out *laughing*, dear – *laughing rapidly*! And pa got nervous, and made the people stand back because he *couldn't think* what that meant, because it never did *that* before, and *might* be going to do almost *anything*! You can't be *sure* of a motor-car; don't you ever have a ride in one, Ethel dear.

And then a punctured hole came in the tyre of the wheel, and something metallic went *click*! And I never knew before that pa could *swear* so dreadfully! Like Major Bullifant, only softer; and I cried. I was so dripping and cold, and all my things spoilt, and I *knew* I'd lost my tennis chance, and that Eva Bell – oh, isn't it cruel and *horrid*! I can't tell you any more about it. I'm going to my room to cry again, and then I shall read 'Paradise Lost' *all the afternoon*. Do come and comfort me, dear. Bring your work and have tea with me, and console your *ever* loving and troubled

MABEL

P.S.– Don't you be *afraid*, dear. Pa shan't take *you* for a ride in the car; besides, he *can't* because the muddy water got into the exhausted valve or something, and it won't work. If it wouldn't ever work any more at all, would it be very *wicked*, Ethel, to be *glad*? Because I'm afraid I should be bad enough to be so *delighted*, you can't think!

As for public transport, the poorer folk of Scalby in those days had to walk to Falsgrave and back to do their shopping, and the children sometimes walked six to eight miles a day going to school and back. For those with means, there was a stagecoach passing between Scarborough and Whitby. What route it took through the district is not known, but at the Hayburn Wyke Hotel there are pictures of the coach pulled up outside. And a large barn to the west of Cumboots Cottages was reputed to have stabled the change-horses.

The regular bus service between Scalby and Scarborough only came about in the third decade of the nineteenth century. Many attempts had been made previously to form an alternative link to the railway, beginning with a horse-drawn wagonette. Presumably this did not pay, for it was soon withdrawn. The old Scarborough Tramway Company suggested running an extension from Manor Road corner to Newby or Scalby, but the

Hayburn Wyke Hotel, still a popular venue for 'pleasure' seekers. Here the Staintondale Hunt meet. Today the hotel no longer boasts a 'Putting Green' of '18 Holes at 3d. a Game'

district council would not sanction the laying of tramlines, though they had no objection to a trolley bus.

After the First World War, two enterprising youths bought an 'army surplus' motor truck, screwed wooden forms down the two sides, and added a canvas cover. One entered or left the vehicle by a little stepladder at the rear. There were no lights inside, so travelling by night could be somewhat of an adventure! Thus came into being the first public motor conveyance between Newby and Scarborough. The single fare was one shilling.

A real passenger bus service was then introduced. It was owned and run by Mr David Allen, and operated as far as Cloughton.

And what of leisure travel? Towards the end of the nineteenth century a new form of transport was designed for pleasure – the charabanc. Several of the Scarborough owners – Jewison, Foxton, etc. – invested in these, and a favourite run out was from Scarborough, through the attractive Forge Valley to Hackness and back via Scalby and Newby. Each vehicle was distinctive and had its individual name like 'Mayflower' or 'Vivid', and was in the charge of a top-hatted driver capable of controlling a four-in-hand.

The original charabanc was built rather high and was inclined to be top heavy, and one overturned when rounding the sweep near Low Hall, where the camber of the road was in the wrong direction. There were several casualties. It took some time to untangle the horses too, with the men kneeling on their heads until the harness could be cut.

A very important person in the cycle of rural transport was the carrier. Hackness and Cloughton had one each, while Scalby had two. In 1905 the carriers were William Johnson and Mrs Sarah Thompson, who possibly took over on the death of her husband. They ran to Scarborough on Tuesday, Thursday and Saturday.[7]

The stock-in-trade was always the same – a covered wagon, complete with horse, a notebook, a good memory and a store of gossip – for it was through the carrier that news was passed from village to village; and if a lift was required, the carrier would always oblige if possible.

Always enterprising, the Edwardian's were quick to exploit the 'travelling shop' idea. Housed in a neat little horse-drawn two-wheeled van, it opened at the rear and the driver would sell from here. The local firm of Wallis & Blakeley. 'Pure Food Specialists', whose main premises were in Newborough, Scarborough, had assistants delivering with handcarts round Scalby when they had a branch shop on Yew Court Terrace until 1926. The company also advertised free trips on the Scarborough trams to customers at their Newborough branch, considered a great innovation at the time.

The butcher, too, was to be seen on his 'rounds', and often had his delivery van enamelled pale-blue inside; he carried a display of knives and saws, with a well-polished steelyard suspended from the interior roof well-hung with joints of meat.

A Mr King, a confectioner in North Marine Road, brought a similar van round Scalby with a cargo of bread and cakes. Fish was usually brought on a handcart, but when the herring fleet was fishing from Scarborough something larger was required, and the vendor would use a horse and cart, while the fishwife chanted: 'Fine herrin', fresh herrin'.' In addition to all these, there were true Romany gypsies, hawkers and pedlars. The last of

The butcher 'going his rounds'. This is thought to be the young Gilbert Cockerill. The Cockerills were butchers in the district for many years, mentioned in a trade directory for 1890. Through the centuries Scalby has been able to boast a variety of tradesmen setting up in the village – wheelwright, stonemason, tailor and draper, blacksmith, market gardener and seedsman (1875), surgeon, land agent, builder, lodging-house keeper (1879), artist, hairdresser, nurse, florist, groom, plumber, fish-hook maker (1840), lapidarist (1823), mariner, engineer, butcher, boot and shoemaker, district surveyor, miller, valuer of farming stock, brick and tile maker, nurseryman, dressmaker and income tax collector!

these making regular visits to the village was 'Scotch Maggie', who carried her basket all the way from Scarborough and always smiled.

The last great transport revolution of the nineteenth century, was the introduction of railways, whose arrival into Scalby heralded its rapid rise as a popular and 'genteel' suburb of Scarborough, and was the one which brought about the most change.

The Scarborough and Whitby Railway Company (S&WR) opened its line between the two towns in 1885. It had been a difficult one to construct, for although only 21 miles long, it included two tunnels – the one under Falsgrave Road, coming out at Gallows Close, the other near Ravenscar on an incline – and the viaduct over the River Esk at Whitby, and a smaller one at Scalby. There were several steep gradients and no opportunity for making a straight line between any two stations. The construction took thirteen years and cost, on average, £27,000 per mile, compared with £6,000 for the York–Scarborough line!

The immediate rail approach to the village, from Scarborough, was over one of the two viaducts, which itself, proved a problem in engineering. Originally of cast-iron construction, it was completed in 1876 by Kirk & Parry, and consisted of seven 35 ft spans and had a total length of 245 ft; but after the collapse of the Tay Bridge, its design was considered too unsafe. It was demolished in 1881 by Waddell's before a single train ran over it, and a brick one was built in its place. A surviving 'Specification of Works' dated 14 February states, 'The viaduct at Scalby shall be carefully taken down and stacked in an approved position upon the Company's property.' It provided for an allowance of £2.00 per linear yard for the 'removal of the old work at Scalby'.

The erection of the second viaduct was almost complete by 1885. The 'Engineers Notebook' gives the quantities and prices for the new viaduct, the total cost of which was £4,188:

Removing old work	£167	Concrete	£181
Excavation	£388	Ashphalte	£32
Concrete foundations	£1081	Ashlar (stone)	£27
Brickwork	£2277	Dry filling	£35

In October 1885, the stonemason who placed the coping on the brick viaduct sued Waddell for the sum of £4 13s. 10d. He had taken on the work as a subcontractor to put the coping on for 8d. a foot for square stones, but had been instructed then to place chamfered stones on to allow for the vibrations of the trains! He claimed for 2d. a foot more for this extra work, but Waddell's counterclaimed for defective workmanship, and won the case, effectively getting out of paying the extra sum.

There seems to have been no difficulty in raising capital for the venture, although the outlook was never considered rosy. Of the eight stations between the two towns only Scalby and Robin Hood's Bay were of any importance, and Burniston, for some reason unknown, decided not to have a station halt.

Another scheme for a branch railway – the Forge Valley Railway of 1873 – would have entailed a junction with the S&WR just short of the south end of the viaduct. The railway line would have then run along the south side of the Scalby 'Cut' to Forge Valley through which it would have passed to its termination at West Ayton.

Station Lane, once little more than a cart-track. It was developed to serve the station and became a 'residential' area in the nineteenth century

The station at Scalby was erected in a somewhat inaccessible place – along a lane that was hardly a road at the time, and a fifth of a mile beyond the outskirts of the village. In spite of this, it proved popular and passenger traffic increased as Station Lane was opened up as a select residential area. It was later taken over by the North Eastern Railway Company.

The Scalby 'Occurrence Book' – compiled by the stationmaster in accordance with regulations laid down – provides some interesting reading. The first recorded incident happened on 29 August 1885: 'Goods Engine off line at the goods yard crossing and was delayed two hours and a half. He arrived here at 9.58 and left at 12.23 and cleared at 12.40, no delay to passenger trains. The stationmaster sent staff with token to Gallows Close and advised platelayers and got the road [meaning rail track] put right'. Staff, it appears, were surprised on 23 July 1893 when, '8.35 am ex Scarbro' arrived here without being signalled'! The timetable, as now, was obviously often subject to alteration and delay without explanation; however on 1 August 1893, the cause was logged, '18 minutes detention to 7.15 am ex Scarbro' attaching van with Sir Charles Legard's otter hounds'.

A serious accident could have occurred on 23 March 1900, when a guard, 'in the act of roping 3 wagons into the siding tripped over rails and fell and did not get the rope off with the result it caught rails and lamp post which it knocked down'.

The goods yard seems to have caused no end of problems for locomotives and footplate staff: 'January 14 1911 – 1.15 pm pilot engine No. 1701, Driver H. Brown, Guard E. Johnson, came off road in Goods Yard (Platform siding) clear of Main Line and switch. Wired Scarbro' for Tool Van but Engine not got on rails until 7.0 pm (no delay to passr. trains). Very sharp curve awkward to get in. Left 8.40 pm after 6.35 pm ex Whitby cleared

Scalby station *c*. 1904 with the picturesque ivy-clad, hump-back bridge whose vegetation once collapsed onto the track in the path of an on-coming train

branch and tablet brought here (only damage one broken rail).' And again on 17 April 1930: 'Engine 1886, Class O derailed all wheels at Catch Points.' A rather more serious accident occurred on 15 January 1942: 'Whilst Goods Motor Driver Ernest Reed and porter N. Heelbeck were unloading Air Raid Shelter plates today the base of Crane broke causing jib to fall and strike Reed on the head – rendering him unconscious. The accident occurred at 11.22 am, the injured man being taken to Scarbro' Hospital by Railway Coys Motor at 11.45 am where he was detained. Approx. 30 cwt of plates were being lowered on to the Motor when the accident occurred.' During a fuel economy drive in 1948, the Railway Executive issued orders for stations to revert to oil lamps – this had little effect on Scalby as only the stationmaster's office had electric lighting!

The variety and amount of goods traffic dealt with by even a small village station was quite remarkable – although some of it, I am sure, staff would rather have been without as a memo to the Pickering Goods Dept. records, dated March 1948:

Horseflesh.– This is still passing in biscuit tins with lids punctured and blood running out at bottoms. Now Summer is approaching the traffic should only be accepted in sealed tins in accordance with regulations. Please approach sender again and point out he has not carried out the promise he made in September last!

Another memo of 1948 relates to the station transport:

Motor Power.– On Tuesday this week I received an order to collect 5 tons of wheat and send it to Manchester Docks. Normally service motor would have done this work on Wednesday but owing to its having to go to Hackness and Langdale End now on that day (owing to road from Forge Valley being blocked) this working was not possible. On Thursday service motor had two days service traffic and could not do it. Yesterday I fully expected doing this job but owing to beer traffic to cellar at Cloughton Motorman found it impossible and telephoned me at 4 pm when I immediately contacted Scarbro' Goods without result excepting permission was given to use service motor today even if overtime was necessary. Now at 12 noon motorman has telephoned to say he has broken down and is being towed home by fitters. Perhaps we may be more fortunate on Monday but if not I will wire yard failing assistance again from Scarbro' as by Tuesday I will have had this order a full week.

A last poignant entry in the Occurrence Book recalls the closure of the station: 'Scalby under Station Master Scarborough Sept 1952 pending closing of Station. Closed officially 28.2.53 – E. Brooks.' Scalby station closed twelve years before the rest of the line, but continued in use as certain trains continued to stop, conveying visitors to the 'Camping Coaches' marshalled on the sidings. The district had proved so popular that it was one of five (of the eight stations) which had camping coaches – Scalby (4), Cloughton (3), Stainton Dale (2), Ravenscar (2) and Robin Hood's Bay (5). Later, part of the station buildings at Scalby and Hayburn Wyke were converted into Camping Cottages when they became unstaffed.

Holidays in these coaches were considered fun if spartan, and because of this occasional complaints were received – one tenant suggesting that his coach was only fit to be burned – bringing a whole new meaning to the British Railway slogan at the time, a 'Holiday to Remember'.

Looking onto the same bridge, with the stationmaster's house on the right

The whole station was demolished in 1974, including the picturesque ivy-clad, hump-backed bridge, and the area was subsequently developed for housing. Today the houses incorporate some of the stonework from the old station, while the trackway itself now provides an idyllic pedestrian route from which to view the delightful countryside around the beautiful village of Scalby.

NOTES

1. Cole, John, *Historical Sketches of Scalby, Burniston & Cloughton*, 1829.
2. Ibid.
3. *The Diaries of Anne Lister (1791–1840)*, ed. Helena Whitbread, Virago Press, 1988.
4. Whellan & Co., *North Riding of Yorkshire Directory*, 1859.
5. Cole, op. cit.
6. Ibid.
7. Kelly's, *North Riding of Yorkshire Directory*, 1905.

Index

MISS BROUGHTON requires experienced Parlourmaids and Cook-Generals, at once, Scarborough and Scalby. Waitresses, Generals able to Cook.– Agency, 35a St Nicholas Cliff. 'Phone 277 [1933].

SCALBY ROAD DISTRICT.– Splendid Detached Residence, with charming garden. Extremely low figure of £975.– Sole Agents, Burkinshaw & Woodcock [1933].

MISS BROUGHTON requires at once Married Couple for Scalby, as Cook and Butler; also Parlour Maids, Cook Generals.– Agency, 35a St Nicholas Cliff. 'Phone 277 [1933].

HOUSES TO LET: Scalby Road, 23/6 and Rates. Also a large selection of self-contained Flats from £65 per annum.– Apply, order to view, Scarboro' Estate Agency, 2 Westborough [1933].

GENUINE CANTERBURY LAMB.– Legs, lions, 1/-; Forequarters, 8d. Prime chilled Beef, top price, 1/- per lb.– Address below.

ALL BACONS are fresh-landed and in perfect condition. No Chinese, Bolshie or other Continental junk sold.– Below.

HENDERSON McKEAN & Co. The Bacon Cutting Experts and Super Quality Butchers, 40 Castle Road, 15 Ranskill Road.

WANTED, Lady Short-hand Typist, with some knowledge of Book-keeping. Permanent post.– State age, wage and experience to John Rowntree and Sons, Grocers, Scarborough [1935].

WARD PRICE.– Scalby village. Detached four-bedroom residence. Perfect order. Open situation. Garage, well laid out gardens. £4,750 [1957].

J. LUCAS GOODALL & SON. Forthcoming Sales. Thursday 31 Jan 1957, at the Central Auction Rooms, Aberdeen Walk. Detached Residence, 'Wynbrook' Scalby with grounds, loose boxes and garages. With Vacant Possession.

GOODALLS.– Overlooking Scalby. Post-war three-bedroom semi. £200 deposit, 54/- weekly [1957].

EDWARD HARLANDS.– Scalby. Brand new 2-bedroom bungalow. Ready June 1957. Complete at £1,850.

EDWARD HARLANDS.– Scalby, residential position. New bungalow, almost ready, two double bedrooms, large lounge, breakfast/kitchen, bathroom. £2,275.

ELLIS & Co.– Scalby. Quietly situated modern post-war semi-detached villa of pleasing design and delightful environment. Lounge, dining-room, three good bedrooms, bathroom, modern kitchen, garage space. Offers £2,750 [1957].

WARD PRICE.– Scalby Mills. Modern three-bedroom semi. Small garden, garage. 80% mortgage available. Close to Sea. £2,050 [1957].

SCALBY VILLAGE. Modern semi-detached villa in this lovely rural atmosphere, 3 bedrooms, lounge and dining room. Roomy kitchen. Bathroom and W.C. Only needs to be seen at this price. £3,200. Stanley Slade & Partners Ltd [1957].

SCALBY VILLAGE. Double fronted, stone built bungalow occupying a unique site with views of the sea, Scarborough Castle and the surrounding countryside. Sheltered position with easily worked garden and grounds of approximately ½ acre with southerly aspect. This bungalow is open to every inspection. Central heating throughout, spacious well-appointed kitchen/breakfast room, bathroom with coloured suite, double garage. Ample room for further bedroom if required. Inspection invited £1,500 or near. W.H. Ellis & Co. [1957].

BURKINSHAW & WOODCOCK.– New bungalow. 1 reception, 2 bedrooms, detached and semi-detached. Scalby, Newby, Cayton. From £1,700 [1957].

WARD PRICE & Co.– Forthcoming Sales (subject to being unsold by Private

Treaty) 24 October 1957. 'Windfall', The Park, Scalby. Detached. Garage. Vacant by orders of executors. 'Farmleigh', North Street, Scalby. Detached Residence. Garage and Outbuildings. Vacant.

EXPERIENCED BUTLER wanted for country house, North Riding of Yorkshire. Modern cottage. Apply with references to Mrs Guthe, Kepwick Hall, Thirsk.

EXPERIENCED MARRIED COUPLE, cook-housekeeper-parlour maid. Country situation on good bus route. Furnished flat available.– Apply Mrs Watson Hall, Scarborough Hall, Driffield.

SCARBOROUGH HOSPITAL.– Ward Maid required, resident or non-resident, full time, permanent post. £6/2/3 for a 48-hour week, plus extra for split duty and Sundays. Part-time cleaner required for mornings, 6 days per week, permanent post. Wage 2/6, 9d–16d per hour.– Applications in writing, and with two names for reference to, Matron, Scarborough Hospital [1957].

VISIT THE EXHIBITION OF A MODEL ELECTRIC KITCHEN For Post-War Homes in the ELECTRICITY SHOWROOMS 89 Westborough, Monday 9th October to Saturday 21st October 1944.

TRANSFER OF MILK REGISTRA-TIONS. Newby and Scalby Area. In consequence of a change of ownership, persons residing in the Newby Scalby Areas who are registered for milk with M & D Hillier, 17 Woodlands Ravine, Scarborough, and Mr W. Hutton, Low Farm, Throxenby, Newby, will have their registration automatically transferred to the new proprietor, Woodlands Dairy Ltd. Commercial Street, Scarborough [1944].